THE GOSPEL OF THE

PRINCE OF PEACE

A Treatise on Christian Pacifism

Other books by Daniel H. Shubin:

Monastery Prisons

History of Russian Christianity
(4 volumes)

Attributes of Heaven and Earth

Kingdoms and Covenants

Leo Tolstoy and the Kingdom of God within You

Skovoroda:
The World Tried to Catch Me but Count Not

Helena Roerich:
Living Ethics and the Teaching for a New Epoch

The Conscientious Objector and the United States Military

THE GOSPEL OF THE PRINCE OF PEACE

A Treatise on Christian Pacifism

Daniel H. Shubin

Peace Church Challenge
Bakersfield, CA

Copyright 2014, Daniel H. Shubin
First Edition
ISBN 978-0-9662757-5-9

Formerly published as:
Militarist Christendom and the Gospel of the Prince of Peace

Email: peacechurch @ jps.net

Table of Contents

1.	Historical Background	9
2.	The Gospel of the Prince of Peace	23
3.	The First Three Centuries	44
4.	Development of Militarist Christendom	69
5.	History of Christian Pacifism	108
6.	American Militarist Christendom	138
7.	Christian Pacifism in America	182
8.	The Dilemma of Militarist Christendom	202
9.	The Contemporary Christian Pacifist	236
	Bibliography	246

DEDICATION

To those who preached the gospel of the Prince of Peace in the recent past and preach it at the present:

Jonathan Dymond
Leo N. Tolstoy
Gerrit Jan Heering
C. John Cadoux
Ray H. Abrams
Jean Lassere
Peter Brock
Guy F. Hershberger
Richard McSorley
John K. Berokoff
John K. Stoner

PART ONE

HISTORICAL BACKGROUND

He (the Messiah) will judge between the nations, and will decide for many people; and they will beat their swords into plows and their spears into pruning shears; nation shall not lift up sword against nation, neither shall they learn war any more.   **Isaiah 2:4**.

1   INTRODUCTION

This book is written by a disciple of Jesus Christ and a student of the Bible for other disciples and students of the Bible. Even if the person reading this book is not a Christian, it will provide an insight into the message preached by Jesus of Nazareth, the Son of God; that the essence of the gospel is the deliverance of humanity from its perpetual self-destructive trend of warfare. This book will also unveil how his message of peaceful coexistence and toleration was transformed into a message of militarism, and how the Apostolic community was transformed into an ecclesiastical political institution. Evidence will also be provided to the reader to testify that the only proper manner for a Christian to conduct himself in the matter of war and military service is to refuse.

Jonathan Dymond wrote in 1847 regarding the purpose of Christianity, and which is just as applicable, if not the more so, today.

> It was the will of God that war be eventually abolished, and Christianity was the means by which this was to occur. Christianity with its present principles and obligations is to produce universal peace. It is because we violate the principles of our religion, because we are not what they require us to be, that wars continue.[1]

These words describe the primary topic of this book: the manner that the gospel message will curb war and military aggression.

At the same time, this book is a history of the development of militarist Christendom and especially the development of the misconception of the militarist Messiah. This includes the manner events and persons of Biblical and ecclesiastical history were interwoven to create an institution that possesses the façade of Jesus Christ, but denies the primary message of the gospel, and which has subjected itself to secular authority for some 1,700 years. As a result, war has progressed generation after generation in Christian countries because the Christian Church as an institution has failed in its obligation to its founder Jesus Christ. All of the information that the author provides in this book is readily available, and to which every student and scholar of Biblical and ecclesiastical history and philosophy has easy access.

2   THE ORIGIN OF LIFE

God is the ultimate creator of life; the parent only transmits life. The state can never be the proprietor of the life of its residents, because the state is made up of people that are likewise created

---

[1] Dymond, Jonathan, *An Inquiry into the Accordancy of War*, pg. 55.

by God. The human, both male and female, is the pinnacle of God's creative process, and this is expressed in the following verse:

> What is a person that You are mindful of him, and the human that You care for him? Yet You have made him a little less than gods, but crowned him with honor and glory. Ps 8:4-5.

No other creature has the characteristics or attributes of the human that so much reflect and retain the same characteristics and attributes of God who created them. The concern of the creator for the human is beyond the ability of the human to comprehend. They are the pinnacle of His creative abilities and each one contains a personal imprint of the hands of the creator Himself. The following passages describe our creation:

> Remember that You have made me of clay, and You will turn me to dust again. Did You not pour me out like milk, and curdle me like cheese? You clothed me with skin and flesh, and knit me together with bones and sinews. You have granted me life and steadfast love; and Your care has preserved my spirit. Job 10:9-12

> Then Jehovah God formed the human from dust from the ground, and breathed into his nostrils the breath of life; and the human became a living soul. Gen 2:7.

> The spirit of God has made me, and the breath of the Almighty gives me life. Behold I am toward God as you are; I too was formed from a piece of clay. Job 33:4,6.

Just as God blew the breath of life into Adam, and he came a living soul, so does God breathe the same spirit of life into every child at the moment it is born and begins to breathe on its own, now a living soul. Since life belongs to God, the human has no right to deprive another person of it. Since God created life, every person is the property of God. Later philosophers, such as Plato, would modify this attitude and declare that the person exists for the benefit of the state, even if it meant that the person had to give up his life in obedience to the dictates of the state.

3   PLATO

The inclusion of militarism in Christendom has its roots in the political philosophy of the Greek philosopher Plato. In his *Republic*, Plato states that the creation of the state as a means of providing for the best interests of its residents is the greatest good.[2] The creation of a class to fight the enemies of the state, and for the sate to expand its borders and enlarge its realm – should the guardians deem it necessary – is treated as an axiom. Residents become the subjects of the state, and are not treated as having individual rights, but are utilized as necessary for the benefit of the state, even if they need to be treated as expendable or as a commodity. The life of an individual belongs to the state, and not to the individual, because the greatest good is the use of the individual to the benefit of the state as dictated by the philosopher-king.

At the same time Plato taught, the god or gods of the state – the supernatural deity – are to be represented such that they are aligned with the good that the state wants to provide its residents. Such a god had the obligation to impress on the warrior it is better to "choose death in battle, rather than defeat and slavery."[3] Plato believed that a nation cannot be strong unless it believes in God; he realized the value of a uniform religion to the stability and success of the military. According to Plato, a mere cosmic force or first cause that was not a person could hardly inspire hope or loyalty or sacrifice, and could not

---

[2] Plato, *Republic*, book 4, 420 b-c, book 5, 471 d-e.
[3] Plato, book 3, 386 b.

offer comfort to the hearts of the distressed, nor courage to embattled souls. Plato taught that a living God could do all this, and advised that the state promote a living God whose doctrines and demands parallel those of the state; religious belief would be used to gain control over the citizens. Plato also taught that control would be more effective if a belief in personal immortality was promoted along with belief in God. This conviction of immortality, the hope of another life, would give the soldiers courage to meet their own death on the battlefield and be able to bear the death of other soldiers and innocent victims.[4]

The propagandists, also known as narrators or poets, had the obligation to provide the residents a god aligned with the interests of the state, which was also to the best good of the residents. According to the text of the *Republic*, no subject or resident would question or doubt that their best interests were at all times in the dictates of the state.

One interesting comment of Plato is the importance that military service plays in the reputation of the state.

> Well, I said, everyone who calls any state courageous or cowardly will be thinking of the part which fights and goes out to war on the state's behalf. No one, he replied, would ever think of any other.[5]

The reason is obvious: the military preserves and expands the civilization as developed by the state. Since this is in the best interest of the state, then the supreme deity likewise approves of the effort of the military in this area. Residents are to be taught to depend on the military as their source of security. Any warrior who abandons the military or resigns due to cowardice is considered a traitor to the state and demoted to a lower rank of service and outside of the armed forces.[6] Those who die in battle are presented the highest honors, as if there was no greater

---

[4] Plato, book 3, 387 d-e.
[5] Plato, book 4, 429 b.
[6] Plato, book 5, 468 a-c.

manner for them to serve their country. It is not in areas of virtue, morality, peace or those areas that develop civilization, such as science or engineering, that are magnified by Plato as significant in the reputation of the state in the world-scene, but the strength and success of the military. The pathetic part is that greater honor is bestowed on soldiers than on reconcilers, and this keeps the tradition of military service at the forefront of civil service.

This allurement or attraction of war and the military profession as described by Plato is repeated by Jonathan Dymond in his book on the causes of war:

> But I believe the greatest cause of the popularity of war,... consists in this: that an idea of glory is attached to military exploits, and of honor to the military profession. Something of elevation is supposed to belong to the character of the soldier; whether it be that we involuntarily presume his personal courage, or that he who makes it his business to defend the rest of the community, acquires the superiority of a protector; on that the profession implies an exemption form the laborious and meaner occupation of life. There is something in war, whether phantom or reality, which glitters and allures; and the allurement is powerful, since we seen that it induces us to endure hardships and injuries, and expose life to a continual danger. The glories of battle, and of those who perish in it, or who return in triumph to their country, are favorite topics of declamation with the historian.[7]

One topic regularly debated is whether Emperor Constantine I may have considered himself the philosopher-king as the pinnacle of sovereign principle, now having defeated his

---

[7] Dymond, Jonathan, *An Inquiry into the Accordancy of War with the Principles of Christianity*, 1870.

enemies, and uniting the entirety of the Roman Empire under a religion superior to that of his predecessors and aligned with the interests of the state, conforming to Plato's *Republic*.

4   SADDUCEES

This section is written in order to present background information on the period that Jesus Christ lived and taught, and also to explain why the Sadducee group of Jews made the statement that Caesar was their king, rather than accepting Jesus as Messiah. From about 6 AD on, the high-priest's office was retained by a small quantity of aristocratic and wealthy Sadducean families. Once having attained this most influential and important plateau in the sacerdotal realm of Judaism, Sadducees were careful not to do anything, or permit anything, which might be to their detriment. They exerted all effort to make sure everything accomplished was in their best interests without incurring any wrath or displeasure of the Roman occupation.

The date of 6 AD is selected because that year Annas son of Seth was appointed high-priest in place of Joazar son of Boethus, and because he became the most powerful of any high-priest of the history of the second temple period, and was the progenitor of the greatest posterity of future high-priests. Anna retained the position 6 to 15 AD, and was the real power behind the position until his death. Subsequent to Annas and until the beginning of the Jewish War in 66 AD, 5 sons, one son-in-law – the infamous Joseph Caiaphas of the New Testament – and one grandson, all held the office. The family of Boethus also provided at least 3 high-priests, and the family of Kanthera at least 2.

The reference in the NT to high-priests in the plural referred to the senior members of the Sadducean families that held the high-priest office at the time. Because of their sacerdotal zeal to resurrect the ancient Levitical and Zadokite priesthood under their own names, Sadducees were the majority of the Sanhedrin on a regular basis, and especially during the ministry of Jesus of Nazareth.

To protect their hard-earned sacerdotal supremacy the Sadducees opposed any popular movement that appeared threatening or that had political overtones. Especially formidable to the Saducean stance was Jesus of Nazareth as Messiah or King, since a claim of this type would cause the suspicion of, and increased oppression by, the Roman occupation, and so undermine the freedoms and power of the Sadducees. This opposition to Jesus' claims of his Messianic office was certainly political, not sacerdotal. The attitude of the Sadducees easily led to the statement of Caiaphas that it would be in the best interests of the Sadducees for Jesus to somehow be eliminated.

> So the chief-priests and the Pharisees gathered a council (Sanhedrin), and said, "What are we to do" For this man performs many signs. If we let him go on in this manner, every one will believe in him, and the Romans will come and destroy both our place and our nation." But one of them named Caiaphas, who was high-priest that year, said to them, "You know nothing at all; you do not understand that it is expedient for you that one man should die for the people, and that the whole nation should not perish." John 11:49-50

The statement of the Sadducees to Pilate culminates their relationship to the Roman occupation.

> They cried out, "Away with him, away with him, crucify him." Pilate said to them, "Shall I crucify your king?" The chief priests answered, "We have no king but Caesar." John 19:125

Sadducees accepted the Romans as the greater power, and the benefactor of sacerdotal freedom and temple authority. If

Sadducees were to recognize Jesus as Messiah, the Roman occupation would deprive them of their freedoms and authority. The Sadducee political institution and social fraternity had no choice except to voice their loyalty, patriotism and acceptance of Roman occupation. To protect themselves, they sacrificed Jesus. As far as the covenant of God was concerned, they had now betrayed Jehovah God in favor of a gentile and pagan king who allotted them superficial earthly gain and the prestige of sacramental ceremonialism.

Jesus was sacrificed in order for the Sadducees to remain in good terms and approval of the Roman occupation, and their fear that the Romans would increase authority and defeat entirely what little of the nation of Israel remained. Jesus became the victim of political expediency, the sacrifice necessary to keep the social order in Judea balanced.

5 WAR AND LOVE IN THE OLD TESTAMENT

The student of the Bible must realize that God dealt with His nation Israel and the other nations of the Middle East in the manner of their culture and era. Their education was meager, science and mathematics and engineering were shallow, and communication was slow. People lived in fear; might was right. Few rules were imposed by God for the success of His people and any others who would take advantage of them, and few rules were provided for their interaction with other nations. God designed the course of history of the 4,000 years from Adam to Jesus Christ taking into serious consideration the barbarism of the people and lack of civilization. God's perfect law included many accommodations due to the uncivilized nature of their society.

The first documented war in the Old Testament is in Gen 14, when the patriarch Abraham armed his servant warriors to defeat 4 alien kings and their armies. Abraham's primarily purpose was to rescue his nephew Lot from these invaders.

Abraham and his small force was the method God accomplished his vengeance on these 4 alien kings for their invasion and pillage of the 5 communities of southern Canaan.

The use of the descendents of Abraham for the execution of God's wrath on the sinful and wicked nations of Canaan is mentioned in a statement of God to Abraham.

> For the iniquity of the Amorites is not yet complete. Gen 15:16.

God was to utilize the arrival of the new nation of Israel to the land promised by God to execute His judgment and penalty upon the indigenous nations of Canaan for their crimes. This is essentially capital punishment on a large scale. The crimes of the residents of Jericho and other areas on both sides of the Jordan River were so serious that God from heaven pronounced them guilty and sentenced them to death. Their execution occurred in their defeat by the armies of Israel, and none was to be spared. Deut 7:1-2. The history of the wars against the Canaanites is documented in the book of Joshua.

God did utilize the nation of Israel to impose penalty on local nations whenever their individual and national crimes increased to some intolerable extent. God pronounced his judgment and sentenced them from heaven, some to slavery, some to death, whatever the proper penalty was that they deserved, and sent His army of Israel to fulfill His command. I Sam 15:1-3. The reverse would also occur when Israel would sin against God. He would summon a local pagan nation to invade Israel and execute the penalty on them. Judg 2:14. This is the history of Israel and the nations of the middle East as noted in the historical books of the Old Testament.

The devastation of the northern kingdom Israel and their deportation to Assyria and Media by the army of Assyria over the course of several years was the judgment of God upon them for their crimes against Him. 2 Kings 17. Likewise God utilized the army of Babylon as His method of executing His penalty on the southern kingdom Judah for their crimes. 2 Kings 24-25. The defeat of Israel and Judah is viewed as penalty on a massive scale for their crimes against one another and against God, and they rightfully deserved such retribution. Such use of the army of Israel in establishing the kingdom and imposing the judgment of God upon the nations was the typical course of national life during the years of the kings of both Israel and Judah, and continued until the war of independence under the forces of the Maccabees.

An indication that a military was not the perfect will of God, but only a temporary accommodation, is evidenced in the reprimand of Samuel prophet when the people of Israel requested a king. I Sam 8. They people wanted a military leader to rule over them and be militarized like the balance of the nations. Although it was not the perfect will of God, he accommodated them and granted their request.

Another incident to be noted is the words of God to King David, that the temple could not be constructed by him because he was a soldier during his career. 1 Chron 28:3. Only a person not contaminated by bloodshed could build the temple, and this was Solomon.

The Old Testament also contains many examples and admonitions of the way of love and non-violence. When there was strife between the herdsmen of Abraham and Lot, Abraham peacefully divided the land between the 2 of them. Gen 13:7-12. When the envious Philistines plugged Isaac's wells, Isaac did not take vengeance, but in a Christ-like spirit he moved to other grounds. Gen 26:12-33. When Joseph was sold into Egypt by his brothers, and after he rose to a position of second ruler in the land, he did not deal with them in the spirit of vengeance, but had an attitude of forgiveness. Gen 43-45. In certain portions of the Old Testament, God's people were commanded to show love to their enemies, for example the command, If you find your enemy's ox or donkey astray, you will surely bring it back to him. Ex 23:4. On one occasion Elisha the prophet took a Syrian army captive, and then fed the men and sent them home. 2 Kings 6:8-

23. These examples prove that God's perfect law was that of harmony and reconciliation between enemies.

6   BIBLICAL JUSTICE

During the Old Testament era capital punishment for a capital crime was legislated by God. To a great extent, these same criteria for determining if a crime deserves capital punishment were transferred over to ecclesiastical law in the middle ages and subsequently into legislated law of western Europe and the Americas.

The purpose of capital punishment was to provide justice to the offended party and those affected by the seriousness of the crime, and also to deter future criminal infraction. Deut 13:5, 10-11. With a speedy trial and conviction by responsible members of the community and their execution of the criminal, crime was to decrease and people would be able to live in greater security.

The initial statute legislating capital punishment is noted in Gen 9:6, for murder, which is defined as a capital crime. Ex 21:12. This was a violation of the fifth commandment, Ex 20:13. Other capital crimes noted in the Old Testament are kidnapping, Ex 21:16. Sorcery, Ex 22:18. False-prophesy, Deut 13:6-11. Premarital sex, Deut 22:20-21. Rape, Deut 22:25. Adultery, Deut 22:24. Necromancy, Lev 20:27. Incest, Lev 20:11-14. Prostitution, Lev 21:9. False-witness in a capital case, Deut 19:15-20. Homosexuality, Lev 20:3. Accidental homicide was not considered murder.

Capital punishment for a capital crime is justice and is classified separately from military combat. To deprive a person of their life was a serious matter and was regulated by the law of God.

7 THE FUTURE MESSIAH

The use of a military to fulfill the objectives of God in imposing His penalty on disobedient nations was only temporary. It had a definite purpose during the ages from the army of Abraham to the army of the Maccabees. The achievement of Jewish independence from the Greeks by the military force under the sons of Mattathias was the final military struggle of the nation Israel. As it began with Abraham their national progenitor, so it ended with the final military king and priest of Israel, Simon son of Mattathias. 1 Macc 15.

The following passages are prophesies of Isaiah, Micah and Zechariah. Each of them prophesied during the later eras of the kingdoms of Judah and Israel. The prophecies quoted here pertain to the Redeemer of Israel, the future Messiah, and deal with the termination of the military of Israel and the transition into a pacifist society at the time of the installation of his reign.

> He will judge between the nations, and will decide for many peoples; and they will beat their swords into plows and their spears into pruning hooks; nation shall not lift up sword against nation, neither shall they learn war any more. Is 2:4. Micah 4:1-3.

> For every boot of the trampling warrior in battle tumult and every garment rolled in blood will be burned as fuel for the fire. For unto us a child is born, to us a son is given; and the government will be upon his shoulders, and his name will be called: Wonderful, counselor, mighty God, everlasting father, prince of peace. Is 9:5-6.

> Rejoice greatly, O daughter of Zion. Shout, daughter of Jerusalem. Behold, your king comes to you righteous and having salvation, gentle and riding a donkey, on a colt the foal of a donkey. I will take away the chariots from Ephraim and the war-horses from Jerusalem, and

the battle bow will be broken. He will proclaim peace to the nations. His rule will extend from sea to sea and from the [Euphrates] River to the ends of the earth. Zech 9:9-10

The new redeemer of Israel, the Messiah, was to install a new type of kingdom or government that would not utilize or have need of a military. Is 2:4 refers to the conversion of the production of factories from weapons and artillery to that of agricultural implements. Military preparation, training and enlistment will terminate in this new kingdom. Is 9:5 refers to the destruction of weapons and armaments.

The Messiah possessing the title of Sovereign of Peace refers to his reign over a kingdom that is not engaged in military service, preparation or conflict. Under the Messiah, the military would desist and the citizens of his kingdom will be adherents of peaceful coexistence with all other nations and nationalities. War will cease to exist in the kingdom of the Messiah.

PART TWO

THE GOSPEL OF THE PRINCE OF PEACE

"My kingdom is not of this world."
Jesus Christ to Pontius Pilate. John 18:36.

8   PURPOSE OF THE GOSPEL

There are many incidents that occurred in the 100 years before the ministry of Jesus Messiah that serve as preliminary events molding the character of discontents in the Jewish nation, that would lead to 2 wars of unprecedented proportions. In the summer of 63 BC, Pompey's entrance into Jerusalem was essentially bloodless and without resistance – the city just surrendered itself to him. It was not as easy to gain control over the temple area. No less than 12,000 Jews died as Pompey's troops captured the temple area and secured it under their control. Thus began the odious Roman military occupation of Judea. Rebellions were regular: in 56 BC under Aristobulus; in 53-51 BC a revolt was led by Pitholaus, where 30,000 Jews were captured and sold as slaves;[8] in 47 BC, a rebellion was led by the robber chief Hezekiah; Herod the Great's siege and storm of Jerusalem in 37 BC, where as many that his soldiers could lay their hands on were murdered; 45 elders executed by Herod in 36 BC; the rebellion against Archelaus in 4 BC shortly after the

---

[8] Schurer, Emil, *A History of the Jewish People at the Time of Christ*, 1st Div. Vol 1, pgg 374-375.

death of Herod the Great; the burning of Sepphoris by King Aretus; and the crucifixion of 2,000 Jews of Jerusalem by Varus, governor of Syria.[9] The Zealots formed their group during this era, an extremely fanatical patriotic group who organized the resistance against Roman occupation.

The leaders selected to govern Judea only increased the odium of the populace, such as the rule of Archelaus, who was tyrannical. He is mentioned in the NT, in the account where Joseph decided to travel directly to Nazareth instead of Jerusalem because of fear. Archelaus had the worst reputation of any of Herod's posterity, and he was so violent that Augustus Caesar deposed him in 6 AD.

Pontius Pilate was governor of Judea during the ministry of Jesus Christ, 26-36 AD, but the contemporary historical account of his rule does not give him any credit. One gospel account mentions that he sent his soldiers to kill some devotees as they were offering sacrifice in the temple. Luke 13:1. As Philo recorded his opinion of Pilate:

> His corruption, his acts of violence, and his rapine, and his habit of insulting people, and his cruelty, and his continual murders of people untried and uncondemned, and his never ending, and gratuitous, and most grievous inhumanity.[10]

As far as the people of Judea were concerned, and their civic and religious leaders, they all agreed on one primary point during the rule of Pontius Pilate, and that was by any means to somehow be freed from the authority of Roman occupation.[11] As a result, the people sought a militarist Messiah to deliver them from Roman military occupation, one who would arrive as a

---

[9] Schurer, Emil, *A History of the Jewish People at the Time of Christ*, 1st Div. Vol 2, pgg 4-5.
[10] Philo, *On the Embassy to Gaius*, (tr. by C.D. Yonge) XXVIII (par. 302)
[11] Schurer, Emil, *A History of the Jewish People at the Time of Christ*, 1st Div. Vol 2, pg 4.

genuine son of King David, and would rid the country of Romans in the same manner that David rid the country of the Philistines. The women sang about King David, how he killed his tens of thousands, and this is the type of Messiah that Judea of that era sought for. They did not want a Messiah who was to tell them to reconcile themselves with the occupation, or to turn the other cheek and suffer offenses, or to put down their weapons, or not get angry with anyone. The Zealots and discontent residents wanted a militarist Messiah, who would gather an army and go to war against the Romans, which they did to their own devastation in the Jewish War of 66-70 AD. Eventually they found him in Simon Bar Kosiba, who was renamed Bar Kochba, Son of the Star, an allusion to Num 24:17, and actually thought he was the militarist Messiah. He was confirmed as their deliverer from Roman occupation by Rabbi Akiva. Bar Kosiba led Judea to their final devastation in the war of 132-135 AD, which was suppressed by Emperor Hadrian.

This leads us to the following conclusion: The primary purpose of the gospel taught by Jesus to his Jewish countrymen was to curb the rebellion and civil war that Jesus realized was going to occur in the future if the Jews continued their enmity against the Roman occupation that they had at present. When the angel appeared to Joseph in a dream and told him to name the future child of Mary Jesus, it was because the child was going to "Save his people from their sins." The sins referred to were the sins of violence against the Roman occupation: vendetta and reprisal for the oppression, execution and enslavement of their residing in Judea. The gospel of the Kingdom was taught in order to turn the discontent populace away from executing vengeance and preparing further revolt and rebellion against the Roman military occupation. As Prince of Peace, Jesus attempted to reconcile the 2 groups: Jewish native subjects and Roman foreign occupiers. The gospel of the Kingdom would then expand to terminate all war, reprisal and aggression on earth for those that would accept Jesus Christ as the Prince of Peace.

In summary, the purpose of the preaching of the gospel of the Kingdom of God and the principles of Christian tenets as taught by Jesus Christ during his ministry was the abolition or elimination of war through either reconciliation between parties, or refusal to participate in violence, reprisal or aggression.

9   THE MESSAGE OF JOHN THE BAPTIZER

The prophesy of Malachi in his final chapter speaks of the time when Jehovah God will send Elijah prophet to the people of Israel before His day of judgment upon them, in order to turn the hearts of the parents to the children, and the hearts of the children to the parents, so that He will not totally destroy them. Mal 4:5-6. No doubt many Jews felt that Elijah in the flesh would appear among the people, or perhaps be reincarnated. Matt 16:14. The words of Angel Gabriel to Zachariah indicate that his son John was to be filled with the spirit of Elijah, and that he would be the one to proceed to reconcile parents and children in Israel. Luke 1:16-17. John's ministry is also described in the song of Zachariah, Luke 1:68-79. He is also called a prophet of God. Luke 1:76. He personally denied that he was Elijah and the fulfillment of the words of Malachi, John 1:21, and in his humility preferred to be identified with Isaiah's lone voice in the desert. Is 40:3. Jesus nevertheless clearly stated that he was Elijah. Matt 11:14.

John the Baptizer was the last of the OT prophets, so his injunction to the soldiers who came to him for divine counsel was in the light of the OT precepts for members of the military: for the soldier not be dishonest or unnecessarily violent, or discontent with their wages. His words, "Do violence to no person," applied to unjust use of force that was so prevalent in occupation armies, who would tend to take advantage of their foreign subjects.

John as a prophet of God had the ability to see distant into the future, to see the result or culmination of the path that the people of Israel were taking. What he saw was the great and terrible day of Jehovah God, His judgment upon Israel for their sins. If the older generation and younger generation were not reconciled, then for sure war would erupt and the nation would be devastated by the Romans. If he did not prepare the people for their acceptance of the Messiah, Jesus of Nazareth, for sure Jehovah would smite the land with a curse. Mal 4:6. This is what the ministry of John Baptizer consisted of: the reconciliation of the generations, for them to abide in harmony with a common goal, and the preparation of the people through the baptism by water for the remission of sins, so they could accept the gospel of the divine kingdom as taught by Jesus Christ and his disciples.

When Pharisees and Sadducees came to him to be baptized, John said to them, "Who warned you to flee from the wrath to come." Matt 3:7. The wrath to come was the devastation John saw in the distant future, defeat and devastation by the Romans, if the people would not repent. In these words John chided the Pharisees and Sadducees, informing them that their self-righteousness served as a hindrance to their repentance. He preached to them in Matt 3:7-10, wanting them to desist in their self-righteous and haughty attitude and to show in their life conduct characteristic of repentant individuals. No doubt John hoped that his message would turn Israel away from the vein of thinking that the population had now been inculcated with for several decades and so alter its course of eventual defeat and devastation.

10   JESUS THE MESSIAH

Violence in previous generations only decimated the population of Israel, devastated the land and brought more tragedy to the nation. The Jews were ill-equipped to defeat a powerful and formidable enemy such as Rome. The manner proposed by Jesus to deliver the nation from devastation was by reconciling the people as individuals with the Roman occupation. Peaceful coexistence was the sole means of the survival of Israel under Roman occupation.

When Jesus said, "Resist not evil," he was not speaking of the general law of retribution for a crime committed. Matt 5:39. Crime must be resisted and dealt with judicially. In this context the words of not resisting evil are followed by the attitude that the soldiers of Roman occupation had toward the Jews: abusing them in public; illegal appropriation of their property; demands of the Jews for transport, food and other services. Jesus was requiring his fellow Jews to be tolerant of this mistreatment by the Roman soldiers, and not seek retribution or vengeance. Eventually the divine kingdom will gain the victory if the Jews place their hope in Jehovah God and not their revolutionary leaders.

When Jesus said, "You have heard that it was said in olden times, Love you neighbor and hate your enemy. But I say unto you, Love your enemies and pray for those who persecute you," (Matt 5:44) he was not referring to any enemy in general, because nowhere in Scripture does it say to hate your enemy. Even when Moses dictates to the people of Israel to annihilate the nations of Canaan he does not utilize the word hate. There was a difference between the necessity of executing the judgment of Jehovah God upon the identified enemy in organized warfare in OT times and the judgment upon a criminal, and the attitude of hate. In reality there is no reason to hate anybody. Hate is an emotion; execution of a criminal is judgment. Regularly David, king and psalm-writer, relates vengeance and retribution on enemies. Ps 41:10. But the explicit statement to hate an enemy is not to be found.

This concept of hating an enemy evolved during the era of the Hasmonaens and their struggle for independence from Greek occupation and Hellenic philosophical invasion. 1 Macc 4:18. This attitude again surfaced with the Roman occupation beginning in 65 BC, and which climaxed under the rule of Herod the Great during the final decade of his life. The freedom fighters and many of the Jewish hierarchy taught the people to hate the

Romans, and which only caused a greater rift between the residents and the occupation forces. This resulted in the massacre of tens of thousands of Jews during the reign of Herod the Great. Jewish children were inculcated with the attitude from childhood that the Roman occupation forces were the enemy and should be hated. Jesus wanted them to change their vein of thinking from that which was prevalent during his era, and so curb further conflict.

When Jesus Messiah told his disciples, "Bless those that curse you and do good to those who hate you," he referring to a change of attitude the Jews must undergo toward the Roman occupation force, if they wanted to avoid total annihilation in the future. Matt 5:44. The victory over the enemy was to be gained by reconciliation. This change of attitude by the Jewish population of Palestine towards the Roman occupation forces would deliver them from their enemies. Luke 1:68-71. The divine kingdom would then flourish in the new divine Israel coincidental with peaceful coexistence. His would materialize as a divine community flourishing within a secular government.

Growing up in Nazareth only 3 miles from the political center of Galilee, the city Sepphoris, and traveling with his father in the carpentry business throughout most of Galilee, Jesus was well familiar with the political unrest of the area. It was in Galilee that violent overthrow was conceived by disenchanted and oppressed Jews seeking independence, and all of this Jesus saw during those years living in Nazareth. He also saw the regiments of Roman troops in rank and file marching down the main roads and highways with their banners, and the armed disciplined soldiers making their presence known to all the residents.

As a prophet Jesus saw in the distant future the annihilation of his people if this course of adverse political action against Roman authority persisted. Even as a young man he heard rumors and no doubt was propositioned with invitations to join such groups, but he early realized that the Romans were no match for the unorganized Jews. The regimented military force of Rome could easily quell any disturbance or even war. These unorganized Jewish splinter groups with their own unstable leadership and lack of cohesion were no match for the well-trained and disciplined ranks of Roman soldiers, who were instilled by their leadership to savage and ruthless war. Cowardice or desertion by a Roman soldier was treason and grounds for immediate and public execution and disgrace of office. The Jews who advocated independence through violent overthrow had no such discipline or organization on such a large scale. Jesus wanted his people to show Romans that there was no intention of violent overthrown, and that the 2 uncommon nationalities could reside in a peaceful coexistence. Jesus wanted Jews to go out of their way to cooperate with Romans to show them they meant them no harm. The few revolutionaries who sought independence from Rome were to cease and desist with a cognizance that the divine kingdom was not to be gained by war and military struggle.

The relative status or relation of the 2 factions was later summarized in the parable noted in Luke 14:31-32. Here Jesus spoke of a king having an army of 10,000 who should first consider whether his military force is enough to defeat another king whose army was 20,000. The wise and intelligent king would send a delegation to conclude a peace treaty rather than risk defeat. With such a peace treaty agreed to by both parties, neither will suffer casualties and property losses. This is to the greatest benefit of the king with the smaller army, who has now secured deliverance of his entire population instead of massive and shameful defeat. This was the intent of this parable to the multitudes. Luke 14:25. Their leaders in Galilee promoting violent overthrow of Roman occupation were the king with the army of 10,000; and the Romans were the army of 20,000. If their countrymen and themselves had any wisdom at all they would seek peaceful coexistence with the Romans. In this manner they would deliver themselves from military defeat and massive devastation.

The purpose of the ministry of Jesus Messiah is disclosed in this parable. It was not armed revolt against the Romans to gain independence, but the effort on behalf of the people to them to conclude a peace treaty, peaceful coexistence with the Romans. This seems to be the most difficult point for Christianity to accept, that the primary reason for the ministry of Jesus as Messiah was to rescue the contemporary and successive generations of Jews from annihilation and the land from devastation by the Roman military. In this manner Jesus Messiah was to rescue his people from their crimes.

This is what Jesus sensed in Judea and foresaw in the near future, 40 years in the distance. The consistent animosity of Jews towards Roman occupation embittered their lives and caused them to develop attitudes of vengeance toward their occupiers. The Roman occupation, to protect itself, increased their suspicion of Jews and executed those they suspected of treason or revolt. Barabbas is an example, who was sentenced to execution for murder, probably killing a Roman soldier during an insurrection. Armed defense and reprisal increased the savagery of the invader and occupation army, and this develops into a vicious cycle, one that Jesus hoped to terminate in Judea by telling his fellow Jews to live in love: peaceful coexistence with the Roman occupation. Although life will be difficult, less lives will be lost. But it was Jewish nationalism that defeated the gospel of the Prince of Peace, and the result was the defeat of the Jewish nation: a million dead, a million taken into captivity, and the devastation of the country in the years 66-70 AD, and total annihilation in 132-135 AD. By refusing the message taught by their Messiah, the Jews crucified Jesus and won the battle – but they lost the war.

11   THE GOSPEL OF THE DIVINE KINGDOM

John the Baptizer first taught the people the good news of the divine kingdom of God. Matt 3:1. After John was committed to prison, shortly after the 40 day fast of Jesus in the desert, Jesus began the proclamation saying, "The time is fulfilled, and the kingdom of heaven is arriving. Repent and believe in the good news." Mark 1:15. The gospel of the divine kingdom was the primary topic of the ministry of Jesus Christ during his 3-1/2 year career. The 12 disciples and later the 70 disciples were sent to preach the good news of the divine kingdom to all the Jews. Matt 10:7. Jesus continued to teach his apostles about the divine kingdom after his resurrection and to the time of his ascension to heaven. Acts 1:3. Apostle Paul taught this gospel throughout his ministry. Acts 28:31. The members of the Messianic assembly at Colossae entered into this divine kingdom. Col 1:13.

This kingdom taught by Jesus is not a material or corporeal government as it existed in Israel in earlier ages, or like the Roman Empire of the era or any other nation. The people accepting the gospel as proclaimed were to repent – turn their life around – and allow God to rule over their life. This would be accompanied by the people being obedient to the code of conduct and morality of the Bible. Jesus said to Nicodemus, that those born of the word (water) and of the Spirit would enter this kingdom. John 3:6.

The divine kingdom materialized on Pentecost among the 120 gathered in the upper room when the holy Spirit descended upon them. With the baptism of the Spirit they spiritually entered the divine kingdom and became its citizens. Although they were in this world, they were members of a realm which had its capital in heaven. Although the disciples of Jesus Christ reside in the world, they are not part of the world. John 17:16. This is a difficult facet of the divine kingdom to be able to grasp: To be in the world, but not of the world.

The establishment of the divine kingdom on this day also meant the fulfillment of the prophesies of Isaiah, Micah and Zechariah among the members of the new kingdom of the Messiah Jesus. (Evidence of this is provided in the section on the Apostolic Fathers.)

The Kingdom of Heaven – or, of God, as in some of the Gospels – transcends the secular states of this world. If a person is a member of this divine Kingdom then he cannot identify himself with the defense or patriotism of the secular states of this world. The present world is temporal and will soon pass away like the change of scenes on a stage, but the Kingdom of Heaven is eternal. This inheritance is presently reserved for us in heaven, and will be revealed at the proper time, at the descent of the holy, heavenly city Jerusalem, our residence for eternity. Why defend a polity or state, then, if it is temporal and if we ourselves are alien from it? The genuine Christian defends the Kingdom of Heaven by testifying to it and refuses to deny it, even if it leads to his own death. The divine kingdom cannot be defended by physical means because it is in heaven, and such a kingdom is unassailable, and so has no need of physical defense. Only the kingdoms of this world require a physical defense.

This is the reason why Jesus reprimanded disciple Peter, who told him not to suffer in Jerusalem. Matt 16:22-23. Peter could not grasp the fact that no matter what should occur to Jesus – even his death – the divine Kingdom is not harmed, because it is unassailable. Even if all the Christians in the world would die as a result of persecution, and all Christian establishments were closed, the Kingdom of Heaven would endure and continue unaffected, because it is unassailable.

The Gospel of the Kingdom of Heaven was preached to the Jews for them to realize that the Messiah came to introduce a kingdom that transcended the secular kingdom that they awaited. To grasp the Kingdom of Heaven, the Jews had to detach themselves from the physical kingdom and transcend it. To place this concept into its historical context, Jesus wanted the Jews to understand the divine concept of the Kingdom of Heaven, that is was not earthly, but heavenly; not secular, but divine. And if they were citizens of a kingdom which was in heaven, no longer would they have a citizenship in their earthly kingdom of Israel or retain patriotism or the need for its defense. This being the cause, there would then be no reason to defend their physical state from Roman occupation and seek a militarist Messiah. Their drive for independence would vanish because something greater would take its place. By accepting the concept of the divine kingdom, reprisal against the Romans would end, and so would the possibility of a civil war, thus fulfilling the words of the angel to Joseph, saving the people from the consequences of their sins. They would no longer consider the Roman occupation their enemy, because only the physical states have enemies, while the enemy of the divine Kingdom is spiritual, it is sin. This is why Jesus said, in reference to the Roman occupation, "Love your enemy," meaning, do not consider the Roman occupation your enemy, because you are citizens of the divine kingdom in heaven.

The same concept applies to the present for genuine Christians who are citizens of the Kingdom of Heaven. They transcend the present secular governments with no obligation to defend the country of their residency from enemies, because these other countries are not their enemy. Other countries are the enemy of the residents who consider themselves citizens and patriots of the physical country, but they are not the enemy of the genuine Christian.

12   THE TESTIMONY OF JESUS CHRIST

When Jesus stood before Pontius Pilate, he was asked if he was a king. Jesus answered in these words, "My kingdom is not of this world." John 18:36. Pilate could not grasp the concept of a person being a ruler over some intangible or incorporeal state or realm. He was perplexed, but then concluded that Jesus was of no threat to his rule as procurator over Judea or to the Roman Empire, and so wanted to free him. The Jews persecuting him likewise could not grasp his message and preferred a militarist king.

That violence is not a solution to a conflict of ideas or physical altercation was exemplified by Jesus Christ when he was arrested by the Roman soldiers.

> And behold one of those [Peter] who were with Jesus stretched out his hand and drew his sword and struck the slave of the high priest, and cut off his ear. Then Jesus said to him, "Put your sword back into its place; for all who take the sword will perish by the sword." Matt 26:51-52.

Jesus followed this reprimand of Peter by healing the wound on the soldier, and then stating that if it was the will of God that he should defend himself from the arresting officers, he could summon Angels from heaven to rescue him. Matt 26:53.

In the Sermon on the Mount, the most studied and applicable passage of the New Testament for disciples of Jesus Messiah, he makes 3 profound statements.

> "You have heard it said of old, Do not kill, and whoever kills will be liable to judgment. But I say to you, that every one who is angry with his brother will be liable to judgment." Matt 5:21-22
>
> "You have heard it said, And eye for an eye and a tooth for a tooth. But I say to you, Do not resist one who is evil. But if any one strikes you on the right cheek, turn to him the other also." Matt 5:38-39.
>
> "You have heard it was said, You will love your neighbor and hate your enemy. But I say to you, Love your enemies and pray for those who persecute you." Matt 5:43-44.

In these passages Jesus forbid his disciples to kill and be violent, or even to become angry. As Messiah of Israel, Jesus perfected the law of God, and taught that no longer was violence, hate, anger, malice, or vengeance to exist among the members of his new church.

Armed combat and military service now terminates with the establishment of the divine kingdom: they are the Church of Christ, the adherents of the New Covenant, the disciples of Jesus Christ. The fulfillment of the prophesies of Isaiah, Micah and Zechariah materialize in the divine kingdom under the Redeemer of Israel, Messiah, Jesus of Nazareth. The concept of Christian pacifism and non-resistance to aggression and violence under the Prince of Peace replaces the military struggle against enemies under the ancient kingdom of Israel, now obsolete. No more are the members of God's people to become involved in the manufacture of weapons and military equipment; this vocation is replaced by those that promote the society and are aimed toward peace and harmony. They are non-violent in every situation and refuse retaliation for offenses or aggression, realizing that there is no justification to violence in any situation, even if means a person's own injury or death.

Jesus Christ said to his disciples, "The disciple is not above his teacher and a servant is not above his master." Matt 10:24. Jesus conducted himself in a non-violent manner when persecuted, and so should his disciples and servants. 1 Pet 2:22-23.

13   THE REAL WAR

For the true Christian, the real war is a spiritual war. It is the war against sin, against the lust of the flesh, and the victory is gained in defeating temptation. Apostle Paul defined it in the following terms:

> Put on the entire armor of God that you may be able to stand against the wiles of the devil. For we do not contend against flesh and blood, but against the principalities, against the power, against the world

rulers of this present darkness, against the spiritual hosts of wickedness in the heavenly places. Eph 6:11-12.

Apostle Paul wrote the letter to the Ephesians during his 2 year imprisonment at Caesarea. Roman soldiers stationed in the prison as sentries, and no doubt an entire regiment or battalion always in training for combat. This led Apostle Paul to utilize the vocation and gear of the secular soldier as an analogy to apply to the real war of the spiritual soldier. The enemy according to Apostle Paul is not flesh and blood, it is not the person on the battlefield. The real enemy is the impulse inside a person that causes him and her to inflict damage and act violently. Sin and lust is the real enemy, and the real victory is gained when temptation is defeated. Apostle James also realized this.

> What causes wars, and what causes fighting among you? It is not your passions that are at war in your members? You desire and do not have; so you kill. And you covet and cannot obtain, so you fight and wage war. Jam 4:1-2.

The apostle Paul described it in the following terms:

> For though we walk in the flesh, we are not waging war according to the flesh. For the weapons of our warfare are not of the flesh but have divine power to destroy strongholds. We destroy arguments and every lofty opinion raised against the knowledge of God, and take every thought captive to obey Christ... 2 Cor 10:3-5

The real war is against the flawed nature of humanity which contains this impulse of aggression and retaliation. The real war is won with faith, the gospel of peace which is reconciliation and with a knowledge of the word of God, knowing how a person should conduct himself. Using these spiritual weapons a person can defend themselves from temptation and gain the spiritual victory.

14   RETROSPECT OF GOSPEL JUSTIFICATION OF WAR

The so-called NT evidence for the justification of war will not be investigated in detail in this volume, because others have already provided ones better than this author could.[12] However, a few passages that pro-war advocates quote will be briefly noted.

In the Sermon on the Mount, Jesus taught his disciples to love their enemies, and this referred to the Roman occupation. The incident of Matt 8:5-13, is a good example of how Jesus put his words into action: Jesus acted charitably to the person who held his people in contempt as political subjects and occupied their territory. The concern of the soldier was his servant, paralyzed and seriously ill, perhaps even near death, and so he, a Roman, was desperate to find someone who would heal him. The Roman soldier was willing to subject himself to a Jewish faith healer – this is probably the manner that the soldier approached Jesus – whom he had heard of: this was the faith that Jesus commended. Jesus as a prophet knew that by commending this faith – or perhaps desperation – of a Roman willing to condescend to a Jew, and by healing the servant, he could display compassion to the soldier and indicate to him that the Jews were not his enemies.

> When Jesus heard him, he marveled, and said to those who followed him, "Truly, I say to you, not even in Israel have I found such faith." Matt 8:11.

---

[12] Bibliography lists these books.

Viewing this statement from the perspective of Jesus' precept to love their enemies, by commending his faith and healing the servant, Jesus displayed love to the enemy of the Jews – the Roman occupation. Jesus overcame evil with good. Rom 12:21. It is obvious that Jesus intended that an act of charity of this type toward the soldier would convince him that the Jews were really not his enemies, and then the soldier would no longer see the need to continue being a soldier and so resign. One of the most quoted passages to defend the military vocation is this comment of Jesus to the Roman centurion, yet its intent is entirely opposite. There is no evidence in this passage that because Jesus complemented his faith, and did not directly reprimand him for his vocation, that Jesus was indirectly approving of, if not at least condoning, his vocation as a soldier in Rome's army.

The same logic can be applied to the visit of Apostle Peter to the home of Cornelius the Roman centurion in Act 10. Peter going to the home of Cornelius and preaching the gospel to him, and them receiving the gift of the Holy Spirit, was the manner that Peter showed love to his enemy: the Roman occupation. Through this act of charity Peter impressed on Cornelius that he was not their enemy, but now, having received the new birth from above, Cornelius and his household were now Peter's brothers and sisters in Jesus Christ. From this point on, Cornelius was to no longer consider either Jews or the members of the new Messianic community his enemy, and he would eventually cease his vocation as a soldier.

That Jesus or Apostle Peter approved of such a vocation as a soldier in commending the faith of the soldier and Cornelius has no more validity than Apostle James approving the vocation of a prostitute by commending the faith of Rahab in James 2:25. This author doubts very much that Rahab continued her business among the people of Israel after her and her family's deliverance from the divine demolition of Jericho.

Slavery is much easier to justify in the NT, with no prohibitions clearly indicated, but on the other hand, having statements by the apostle Paul for the proper treatment of slaves by slave owners: Titus 2:9, Eph 6:5, and I Cor 7:21. The entire book of Philemon deals with Apostle Paul returning a runaway slave Onesimus to his master, and nowhere in this book is the institution of slavery condemned or discredited. Not one passage in the NT requires slave owners to free their slaves upon becoming Christian! The trend of Apostolic thinking to eventually result in the emancipation of slaves is exemplified in Gal 3:28 and Col 3:11, that the slave and slave owner are equal in the eyes of God. Eventually, the apostle hoped that Christian love would initiate emancipation.

Herding animals out of the temple area can hardly be utilized as a comparable event to the vocation of a soldier and the practice and atrocities of warfare. John 2:14, Matt 21:12. The whip used by Jesus was made of the ropes that tied to cattle together. Apparently, Jesus first untied the cattle, then used the ropes to herd them out of the temple premises. As Messiah, Jesus had the right to reprimand those who corrupted the true worship of God in his Father's house. Jesus impressed on the Sadducees their corruption of temple worship by upsetting the tables of the money changes and driving out the sacrificial animals for sale. In each case they ignored him and shortly after continued their business practices. The point of discussion applicable is whether Jesus would have defended himself if attacked by these religious criminals. He would not have, just as he did not defend himself when arrested.

The final passage to be discussed is the statement of Jesus to his disciples just prior to leaving the Passover for the garden of Gethsemane.

> And they said, "Look Lord, here are two swords." And
> he said to them, "It is enough." Luke 22:38.

If Jesus really thought that 2 swords were enough to defend him, he was far from right. Viewing the incident objectively, what good would only 2 swords serve among 12 of them against a crowd of soldiers and temple servants who had swords and clubs.

To think that Jesus felt 2 swords were enough to defend him against his arrest is ludicrous. The passage of Luke 22:35-38 requires interpretation as an allegory, interpreted in the light of the use of swords in similar passages, such as Matt 10:34-35, Luke 2:35, Eph 6:17, and Heb 4:12. As Jean Lassere interpreted the incident:

> By solemnly commanding them to take a purse, a scrip, and a sword, He wanted to make them understand through striking imagery that the hour had come for them to prepare themselves for a tragic spiritual battle. They would need a supply of moral forces and a spiritual pugnacity to help them overcome the ordeal of their dispersion and the despair in which He would leave them by His death. For then each of them could count on his own resources alone.[13]

Jean Calvin likewise provided a similar conclusion:

> It was truly shameful and stupid ignorance that the disciples, after having been so often informed about bearing the cross, imagine that they must fight with *swords* of iron. When they say that they have *two swords,* it is uncertain whether they mean that they are well prepared against their enemies, or complain that they are ill provided with arms. It is evident, at least, that they were so stupid as not to think of a spiritual enemy.[14]

That the disciples misinterpreted Jesus statement to sell their mantle and purchase a sword is evidenced when one of the disciples, Peter, actually used the sword to defend Jesus when the soldiers attempted to arrest him.

---

[13] Lassere, Jean, *War and the Gospel*, pg. 42.
[14] Calvin, Jean, *Commentaries*, Luke 22:38

> And behold one of those [Peter] who were with Jesus stretched out his hand and drew his sword and struck the slave of the high priest, and cut off his ear. Then Jesus said to him, "Put your sword back into its place; for all who take the sword will perish by the sword." Matt 26:51-52.

Jesus followed this reprimand of Peter by healing the wound on the soldier, and then stating that if it was the will of God that he should defend himself from the arresting officers, he could summon Angels from heaven to rescue him. Matt 26:53

The law was superceded by the gospel, however, because of necessity, militarist Christendom grasps one of the tenets that were made obsolete by the death and resurrection of Jesus and utilizes every passage in the NT to prove that it has not been abolished. The several statements of Jesus in the Sermon on the Mount, where the old law was replaced by a new mode of conduct that contain the phrase, "You have heard it said of old,... but I say unto you,..." likewise pertain to war, reprisal and violent aggression. Christendom dismisses Moses and the laws of his dispensation to justify Christian freedom, except in the case of Christian freedom from war. Then Christendom applies the OT with full force as its justification, even though the general trend of the gospel is that of peace and reconciliation and endurance of offense and abuse without reprisal.

To use human weakness as an excuse to not observe the command to not be angry with your brother, or not to turn the other cheek, is no different than using the same excuse to violate any other command of God, which ever one it might be. If we are unable to observe the command then it is our attitude we should change, not the gospel. We should pray for the strength to follow in the footsteps of Jesus and not revile in return when we are reviled, not threaten in return when we are threatened, and die to sin and live to righteousness. If we are unable to turn the other cheek, put down that weapon, not become angry with someone, love our enemy, and suffer even unto death, the problem is not with the commands of Jesus, but with us, and we must change our attitude through prayer and fasting and penance to conform to his example.

PART THREE

THE FIRST THREE CENTURIES

For we no longer take up sword against nation, nor do we learn war any more, having become children of peace, for the sake of Jesus, who is our leader...
Origen[15]

15   THE APOSTOLIC PERIOD

During the initial 150 years after the ministry of Jesus Christ the members of the newly-formed Christian churches, or Messianic communities as they rightly should be called, abstained from combat and military service. The earliest of these were the Messianic Jews of the apostolic period. These Jews fled Judea to the east side of the Jordan River by prophecy to escape the invasion of Judea by the Roman army, the Jewish War and the devastation of the country, which occurred in the years 66-70 AD. Their migration fulfilled the prophecy of Dan 11:41. The Jewish Christians of Judea were delivered from catastrophe on the east side of the Jordan River and Dead Sea, according to Eusebius, the church historian. None of the Messianic Jews joined the Jewish revolutionaries or took up arms to defend their country from invasion by the Roman army or in the defense of Jerusalem during the siege.[16]

---

[15] *Against Celsus*, 5:33
[16] Eusebius, *Ecclesiastical History*, book 3, chapter 5.

The group that fled Judea to Pella just prior to the Jewish War of 66-70 AD were known as the Ebionites, who were the original Messianic Jews. They adhered to Jesus' gospel and refused to join the Jewish groups to fight the Roman occupiers. Subsequent to the Ebionites arose the Nazarenes, who spread north into Syria and existed until the fourth century. Although the Ebionites and Nazarenes were accused of being legalistic, nonetheless, they were pacifist, having accepted the gospel directly from Jesus Messiah and his immediate listeners and disciples. After the final defeat of Jerusalem under Hadrian in the war of 132-135 AD, and the conversion of the city into the Roman Aelia Capitolina, some of the Nazarenes were able to return to the city as Christians and not as Jews and resettled there. Edward Gibbon noted the following regarding these earliest of Christians:

> Their simplicity was offended by the use of oaths, by the pomp of magistracy, and by the active contention of public life; nor could their humane ignorance be convinced that it was lawful on any occasion to shed the blood of our fellow-creatures, either by the sword of justice, or by that of war; even though their criminal or hostile attempts should threaten the peace and safety of the whole community. It was acknowledged, that, under a less perfect law, the powers of the Jewish constitution had been exercised, with the approbation of Heaven, by inspired prophets and by anointed kings. The Christians felt and confessed that such institutions might be necessary for the present system of the world, and they cheerfully submitted to the authority of their Pagan governors.
> But while they inculcated the maxims of passive obedience, they refused to take any active part in the civil administration or the military defense of the empire. Some indulgence might, perhaps, be allowed to those persons who, before their conversion, were already

engaged in such violent and sanguinary occupations; but it was impossible that the Christians, without renouncing a more sacred duty, could assume the character of soldiers, of magistrates, or of princes. This indolent, or even criminal disregard to the public welfare, exposed them to the contempt and reproaches of the Pagans who very frequently asked, what must be the fate of the empire, attacked on every side by the barbarians, if all mankind should adopt the pusillanimous sentiments of the new sect. To this insulting question the Christian apologists returned obscure and ambiguous answers, as they were unwilling to reveal the secret cause of their security; the expectation that, before the conversion of mankind was accomplished, war, government, the Roman empire, and the world itself, would be no more.

It may be observed, that, in this instance likewise, the situation of the first Christians coincided very happily with their religious scruples, and that their aversion to an active life contributed rather to excuse them from the service, than to exclude them from the honors, of the state and army.[17]

If we seriously consider the purity of the Christian religion, the sanctity of its moral precepts, and the innocent as well as austere lives of the greater number of those who during the first ages embraced the faith of the gospel, we should naturally suppose, that so benevolent a doctrine would have been received with due reverence, even by the unbelieving world; that the learned and the polite, however they may deride the miracles, would have esteemed the virtues, of the new sect; and that the magistrates, instead of persecuting, would have protected an order of men who yielded the

---

[17] Gibbon, Edward *Decline and Fall of the Roman Empire*, vol 1, chapter 15, part 5.

most passive obedience to the laws, though they declined the active cares of war and government.[18]

Other historians note the following:

> For the first three centuries, no Christian writing which has survived to our time condoned Christian participation in war.[19]

> But as a matter of fact, there is no trace of the existence of any Christian soldiers between these cases mentioned in Acts and say, 170 AD.[20]

> It is thus not surprising that there was no military question in the congregations until roughly the time of Marcus Aurelius.[21] The baptized Christians did not become a soldier, and those who were converted to the Christian faith in the camp had to determine how they might come to terms with their soldier's life.[22]

All available testimony regarding the earliest of Christians – both Jewish and gentile – prevails in indicating that the members of the original Messianic communities refused to be part of the Roman military, as well as government in general. The reasons for the vocation of a soldier being offensive to a Christian are very apparent when comparing the Christian teaching to the expected responsibilities of a soldier: Christianity on principle rejected war and bloodshed; the soldiers would have to execute criminals; the unconditional oath of the soldier that the supreme authority was the Emperor was in conflict with sole allegiance to the God and Father of Jesus Christ; the cult of the

---

[18] Gibbon, vol 1, chapter 16, part 1.
[19] Latourette, K.C., *A History of Christianity*, Vol. 1, pg. 242-243.
[20] Cadoux, C. John, *The Early Christian Attitude toward War*, pg. 229.
[21] Roman Emperor, 161-180 AD.
[22] Harnack, Adolf, *Militia Christi*, pg. 69.

emperor was strong in the armed forces and no soldier could avoid it; sacrifices to pagan gods were regularly offered by officers, and soldiers were required to participate; the military standards were identified with pagan deities and the emperor; the general conduct of soldiers conflicted with the high moral standards of the NT; the soldiers participated in various festivals, parades and amusements that deviated from the NT teaching.[23]

The first notice of a person professing to be Christian that was in the service of the Roman military was about 150 years after Jesus Christ concluded his ministry, and they were vehemently censured for it, and it was another 150 years before any writer or apologist who was a professing Christian condoned the profession of a soldier in the Roman army. These men who were in the military in about 170 AD, based on the evidence that is available, were baptized into the religion while still soldiers, but were not required to leave their military vocation by the local bishop or congregation. The most probable reason was that no war was in progress at the time, and the bishop was morally too weak to require the novitiate's resignation or the novitiate felt no reason to resign.

However it was during this same period that Tertullian wrote his several treatises against Roman military service, and so did Irenaus, Clement of Alexandria, Origin and Cyprian. No doubt they had heard of professing Christian novitiates who were soldiers and who saw no need to resign from their vocation as a professional soldier, and especially in time of peace. The compromise with the state began at the local parish level, which motivated the apologists to refute the compromise immediately with their treatises, lest the practice further spread to other parishes and other morally weak bishops.

The evidence provided by the apologists of the ante-Nicene era, from the beginning of the 2nd century to the early 4th century, indicates that the Christian religion was different than

---

[23] Harnack, pg. 65.

the balance of religions and philosophies in the Roman Empire in its attitude towards war and military service. They identified the insignias, flags, oaths, and practices of the military with pagan and idolatrous rites. The conduct of military personal in peacetime was corrupt, amoral and obscene, while in war it was the most inhumane and barbaric, no different than our present era.

The gospel the apologists received from the apostles and their direct spiritual descendents was that the cessation of war and its preparation was fulfilled in Jesus Christ, and that a renouncement of military service was required for the members of the Christian church. This attitude was not retained easily by the Christian of early centuries and especially due to persecution. Some Christians succumbed to the pressure of the military and accepted service, and their history is also noted in the annals of the apologists. Persecution against Christians occurred regularly in the Roman Empire and many who refused military service were executed. The worst of the persecutions was under Diocletian, beginning 303 AD, and until 312 AD.

The following are excerpts from the apologists of the 2nd and 3rd century. They reflect the attitudes and practices of Christians during the early centuries prior to the Council of Nicea. Not every writer of the period will be mentioned, and not every passage dealing with this topic from the writers selected, but only the more influential and popular. The authors are also from various segments of the Roman Empire, including North Africa, Europe and Middle East. This will provide sufficient evidence of the conscientious objection nature and attitude of the Christian churches of the first three centuries.

16 TERTULLIAN

The primary witness to the exclusion of early followers and disciples of the teachings of Jesus to military conscription is Tertullian. He was also a Montanist during part of his life, and would have inherited his conviction from them regarding Christian pacifism. He was the first of the great Latin apologists, writing 160-220 AD, having his center of ministry in northern Africa. The following passage is from Tertullian's treatise *On Idolatry*.

> Chapter XIX. - Concerning Military Service.
>
> In that last section, decision may seem to have been given likewise concerning military service, which is between dignity and power. But now inquiry is made about this point, whether a believer may turn himself unto military service, and whether the military may be admitted unto the faith, even the rank and file, or each inferior grade, to whom there is no necessity for taking part in sacrifices or capital punishments. There is no agreement between the divine and the human sacrament, the standard of Christ and the standard of the devil, the camp of light and the camp of darkness. One soul cannot be due to two masters-God and Caesar. And yet Moses carried a rod, and Aaron wore a buckle, and John (the Baptizer) is girt with leather and Joshua the son of Nun leads a line of march; and the People warred: if it pleases you to sport with the subject. But how will a Christian man war, nay, how will he serve even in peace, without a sword, which the Lord has taken away? For albeit soldiers had come unto John, and had received the formula of their rule; albeit, likewise, a centurion had believed; still the Lord afterward, in disarming Peter, disarmed every soldier. No uniform is lawful among us, if assigned to any unlawful action.[24]

The introductory paragraph to the *De Chaplet or Corona* (*Treatise on the Crown*) is a narrative of a soldier who can no

---

[24] Ante-Nicene Fathers, vol. 3, pg. 99-100

longer be a member of the Roman military. More than likely, and in the tradition of the Roman military, he was executed for desertion.

Chapter I.
Very lately it happened thus: while the bounty of our most excellent emperors was dispensed in the camp, the soldiers, laurel-crowned, were approaching. One of them, more a soldier of God, more steadfast than the rest of his brethren, who had imagined that they could serve two masters, his head alone uncovered, the useless crown in his hand-already even by that peculiarity known to every one as a Christian-was nobly conspicuous. Accordingly, all began to mark him out, jeering him at a distance, gnashing on him near at hand. The murmur is wafted to the tribune, when the person had just left the ranks. The tribune at once puts the question to him, Why are you so different in your attire? He declared that he had no liberty to wear the crown with the rest. Being urgently asked for his reasons, he answered, I am a Christian. O soldier! boasting thyself in God. Then the case was considered and voted on; the matter was remitted to a higher tribunal; the offender was conducted to the prefects. At once he put away the heavy cloak, his disburdening commenced; he loosed from his foot the military shoe, beginning to stand upon holy ground; he gave up the sword, which was not necessary either for the protection of our Lord; from his hand likewise dropped the laurel crown; and now, purple-clad with the hope of his own blood, shod with the preparation of the gospel, girt with the sharper word of God, completely equipped in the apostles' armor, and crowned more worthily with the white crown of martyrdom, he awaits in prison the largess of Christ.[25]

The following is chapter 11 from the *Treatise on the Crown*.

Chapter XI.
To begin with the real ground of the military crown, I think we must first inquire whether warfare is proper at all for Christians. What sense is there in discussing the merely accidental, when that on which it rests is to be condemned? Do we believe it lawful for a human oath to be superadded to one divine, for a man to come under promise to another master after Christ, and to abjure father, mother, and all nearest kinsfolk, whom even the law has commanded us to honor and love next to God Himself, to whom the gospel, too, holding them only of less account than Christ, has in like manner rendered honor? Shall it be held lawful to make an occupation of the sword, when the Lord proclaims that he who uses the sword shall perish by the sword? And shall the son of peace take part in the battle when it does not become him even to sue at law? And shall he apply the chain, and the prison, and the torture, and the punishment, who is not the avenger even of his own wrongs? Shall he, forsooth, either keep watch-service for others more than for Christ, or shall he do it on the Lord's day, when he does not even do it for Christ Himself? And shall he keep guard before the temples which he has renounced? And shall he take a meal where the apostle has forbidden him? And shall he diligently protect by night those whom in the day-time he has put to flight by his exorcisms, leaning and resting on the spear the while with which Christ's side was pierced? Shall he carry a flag, too, hostile to Christ? And shall *he* ask a watchword from the emperor who has already received one from God? Shall *he* be disturbed in death by the

---

[25] Ante-Nicene Fathers, vol. 3, pg. 99-100

trumpet of the trumpeter, who expects to be aroused by the angel's trump? And shall the Christian be burned according to camp rule, when he was not permitted to burn incense to an idol, when to him Christ remitted the punishment of fire? Then how many other offences there are involved in the performances of camp offices, which we must hold to involve a transgression of God's law, you may see by a slight survey. The very carrying of the name over from the camp of light to the camp of darkness is a violation of it. Of course, if faith comes later, and finds any preoccupied with military service, their case is different, as in the instance of those whom John used to receive for baptism, and of those most faithful centurions, I mean the centurion whom Christ approves, and the centurion whom Peter instructs; yet, at the same time, when a man has become a believer, and faith has been sealed, there must be either an immediate abandonment of it, which has been the course with many; or all sorts of quibbling will have to be resorted to in order to avoid offending God, and that is not allowed even outside of military service; or, last of all, for God the fate must be endured which a citizen-faith has been no less ready to accept. Neither does military service hold out escape from punishment of sins, or exemption from martyrdom. Nowhere does the Christian change his character. There is one gospel, and the same Jesus, who will one day deny every one who denies, and acknowledge every one who acknowledges God, who will save, too, the life which has been lost for His sake; but, on the other hand, destroy that which for gain has been saved to His dishonor.[26]

Tertullian felt the allegiance given to the state through the military oath to defend the nation against all enemies as defined

---

[26] Ante-Nicene Fathers, vol. 3, pg. 99-100

by their Senate to be disloyal to the true God. The oath would have included a testimony of obedience to the Roman Emperor, likewise repulsive to Tertullian. The flag or banner carried by the troops was antithesis to the spiritual signs and character traits of true Christians, and in general, all that the military entailed was antithesis to the teachings of Jesus Christ. Tertullian also mentions that soldiers who become Christians while in the military resigned themselves from that vocation.

17   CYPRIAN

Cyprian, known to be a disciple of Tertullian likewise wrote in several passages that involvement in war was unacceptable to Christians as well as unjust and hypocrisy. The following is an excerpt from his Epistles.

> The whole world is wet with mutual blood; and murder, which in the case of an individual is admitted to be a crime, is called a virtue when it is committed wholesale.[27]

Cyprian claims that it is hypocrisy to proclaim as a hero and valiant the person who will destroy and devastate the life and property of innocent people in organized warfare, when it is considered a crime if the same occurs in peacetime.

18   JUSTIN OF CAESAREA

One of the earliest apologists was Justin of Caesarea, often titled, Justin Martyr. He wrote about the years 140 to 160 AD, during the era when those who were taught by the apostles transmitted the gospel to his – the next – generation, and which

---

[27] Ante-Nicene Fathers, vol. 5, pg. 277

original gospel was still untainted by later Greek philosophy and anti-Semitism.

Justin taught that the prophecy of Is 2:4 was fulfilled in the gospel preached by the 12 apostles, and so they ceased any involvement in war and military service. This he mentions in his *First Apology*, chapter 39:

> And when the Spirit of prophesy speaks as predicting things that are to come to pass, He speaks in this way, "For out of Zion shall go forth the law, and the word of the Lord from Jerusalem. And He shall judge among the nations, and shall rebuke many people; and they shall beat their swords in to ploughshares, and their spears into pruning hooks; nations shall not lift up sword against nation, neither shall they learn war any more.:" And that it did so come to pass, we can convince you. For from Jerusalem there went out into the world, men, twelve in number, and these illiterate, of no ability in speaking; but by the power of God they proclaimed to every race of men that they were sent by Christ to teach to all the word of God; and we who formerly used to murder one another do not only now refrain from making war upon our enemies, but also, that we may not lie nor deceive our examiners, willingly die confessing Christ.[28]

A similar definition of the fulfillment of Isaiah's prophetic words in the Messianic communities is mentioned in his *Dialogue with Trypho*, chapter 50.

> And we who were filled with war, and mutual slaughter, and every wickedness, have each through the whole earth changed our warlike weapons, - our swords into ploughs, and our spears into implements of tillage, - and

---

[28] Ante-Nicene Fathers, vol. 1, page 175-176

we cultivate piety, righteousness, philanthropy, faith, and hope, which we have from the Father Himself through Him who was crucified.[29]

In both these passages Justin indicates that the Christians of his era felt the era of military service to conclude, and the new era of pacifism to inaugurate, with the Messiah Jesus.

19   HYPPOLYTUS

Another early witness to Christian refusal to war and military service is the 16th Canon of the Apostolic Tradition of Hyppolytus (170-236 AD), which was composed about 215 AD in Rome:

> 16. Inquiry shall likewise be made about the professions and trades of those who are brought to be admitted to the faith. If a man is a panderer, he must desist or be rejected. If a man is a sculptor or painter, he must be charged not to make idols; if he does not desist he must be rejected. If a man is an actor or pantomimist, he must desist or be rejected. A teacher of young children had best desist, but if he has no other occupation, he may be permitted to continue. A charioteer, likewise, who races or frequents races, must desist or be rejected. A gladiator or a trainer of gladiators, or a huntsman [in the wild beast shows], or anyone connected with these shows, or a public official in charge of gladiatorial exhibitions must desist or be rejected. A heathen priest or anyone who tends idols must desist or be rejected. A soldier of the civil authority must be taught not to kill men and to refuse to do so if he is commanded, and to refuse to take an oath; if he is unwilling to comply, he must be rejected. A military commander or civic

---

[29] Ante-Nicene Fathers, Vol. 1, page 254

magistrate that wears the purple must resign or be rejected. If a catechumen or a believer seeks to become a soldier they must be rejected, for they have despised God. [30]

This section deals with the professions that are not acceptable practice for Christians, and which a newly-converted Christian must resign from in order to be admitted into the local Church.

20   IRENAEUS

Irenaeus had his home in southern Gaul, modern France, although he also spent much time in Rome. His writings were primarily directed against the prevalent heresy of Gnosticism during the era of 180-190 AD. The following is an except from his treatise *Against Heresies*, 4:34:4.

> But preached by the apostles – who went forth from Jerusalem – throughout all the earth, caused such a change in the state of things, that these [nations] did form the swords and war-lances into plows, and changed them into pruning hooks for reaping the corn, that is, into instruments used for peaceful purposes, and that they are now unaccustomed to fighting, but when smitten, offer the other cheek. [31]

This excerpt follows the same vein of Justin that the words of Isaiah were fulfilled in the gospel taught by Jesus Christ, and which new mode of conduct was accepted by the gentiles of the Roman Empire.

---

[30] Hyppolytus, *Apostolic Tradition*, part 2, section 16.
[31] Ante-Nicene Fathers, Vol. 1, page 512

21 CLEMENT OF ALEXANDRIA

Clement taught in Alexandria, Egypt, and wrote about 190-210 AD. He inclines toward pacifism as a character trait of the Christian. The following is a passage from Clement's *Instructor*, book 1, chapter 12.

> For it is not in war, but in peace, that we are trained. War needs great preparation, and luxury craves profusion; but peace and love, simple and quiet sisters, require no arms, nor excessive preparation. The Word is their sustenance.[32]

22 ORIGEN

Origen in several passages mentions pacifism as a trait of the Christians. These are primarily located in his treatise *Against Celsus*.

> And yet, if a revolt had led to the formation of the Christian commonwealth, so that it derived its existence in this way from that of the Jews, who were permitted to take up arms in defense of the members of their families, and to slay their enemies, the Christian Lawgiver would not have altogether forbidden the putting of men to death; and yet He nowhere teaches that it is right for His own disciples to offer violence to any one, however wicked. For He did not deem it in keeping with such laws as His, which were derived from a divine source, to allow the killing of any individual whatever.[33] (*Against Celsus*, 3:7)

---

[32] Ante-Nicene Fathers, vol. 2, pg. 234-235
[33] Ante-Nicene Fathers, vol. 4, pg. 467

But with regard to the Christians, because they were taught not to avenge themselves upon their enemies (and have thus observed laws of a mild and philanthropic character); and because they would not, although able, have made war even if they had received authority to do so,--they have obtained this reward from God, that He has always warred in their behalf, and on certain occasions has restrained those who rose up against them and desired to destroy them.[34] (*Against Celsus*, 3:8)

And to those who inquire of us whence we come, or who is our founder, we reply that we are come, agreeably to the counsels of Jesus, to cut down our hostile and insolent wordy swords into plows, and to convert into pruning-hooks the spears formerly employed in war. For we no longer take up sword against nation, nor do we learn war any more, having become children of peace, for the sake of Jesus, who is our leader, instead of those who our fathers followed, among whom we were strangers to the covenant.[35] (*Against Celsus*, 5:33)

In the next place, Celsus urges us "to help the king with all our might, and to labor with him in the maintenance of justice, to fight for him; and if he requires it, to fight under him, or lead an army along with him." To this our answer is, that we do, when occasion requires, give help to kings, and that, so to say, a divine help, "putting on the whole armor of God." And this we do in obedience to the injunction of the apostle, "I exhort, therefore, that first of all, supplications, prayers, intercessions, and giving of thanks, be made for all men; for kings, and for all that are in authority;" and

---

[34] Ante-Nicene Fathers, vol. 4, pg. 467-468
[35] Ante-Nicene Fathers, vol. 4, pg. 558

the more any one excels in piety, the more effective help does he render to kings, even more than is given by soldiers, who go forth to fight and slay as many of the enemy as they can. And to those enemies of our faith who require us to bear arms for the commonwealth, and to slay men, we can reply: "Do not those who are priests at certain shrines, and those who attend on certain gods, as you account them, keep their hands free from blood, that they may with hands unstained and free from human blood offer the appointed sacrifices to your gods; and even when war is upon you, you never enlist the priests in the army. If that, then, is a laudable custom, how much more so, that while others are engaged in battle, these too should engage as the priests and ministers of God, keeping their hands pure, and wrestling in prayers to God on behalf of those who are fighting in a righteous cause, and for the king who reigns righteously, that whatever is opposed to those who act righteously may be destroyed!" And as we by our prayers vanquish all demons who stir up war, and lead to the violation of oaths, and disturb the peace, we in this way are much more helpful to the kings than those who go into the field to fight for them. And we do take our part in public affairs, when along with righteous prayers we join self-denying exercises and meditations, which teach us to despise pleasures, and not to be led away by them. And none fight better for the king than we do. We do not indeed fight under him, although he require it; but we fight on his behalf, forming a special army--an army of piety--by offering our prayers to God.[36] (*Against Celsus*, 8:73)

---

[36] Ante-Nicene Fathers, vol. 4, pg. 667-668

In every passage dealing with this topic, Origen makes is clear that war and military service was abrogated by Jesus Christ, and that Christians of his era refused to take up arms under any circumstance. Origen acknowledges that war was permitted in OT times, but now under the New Covenant, this is no longer permitted.

23   ARNOBIUS

The treatise of Arnobius *The Seven Books against the Heathen*, testifies further to Jesus' fundamental precept of prohibition of violence and bloodshed, and the preference to suffer offense, rather than to take vengeance. Arnobius further states that if all people would grasp this principle, harmony would prevail in the world. The following is a selection from Book 1:

> 6. Although you allege that those wars which you speak of were excited through hatred of our religion, it would not be difficult to prove, that after the name of Christ was heard in the world, not only were they not increased, but they were even in great measure diminished by the restraining of furious passions. For since we, a numerous band of men as we are, have learned from His teaching and His laws that evil ought not to be requited with evil, that it is better to suffer wrong than to inflict it, that we should rather shed our own blood than stain our hands and our conscience with that of another, an ungrateful world is now for a long period enjoying a benefit from Christ, inasmuch as by His means the rage of savage ferocity has been softened, and has begun to withhold hostile hands from the blood of a fellow-creature. But if all without exception, who feel that they are men not in form of body but in power of reason, would lend an ear for a

little to His salutary and peaceful rules, and would not, in the pride and arrogance of enlightenment, trust to their own senses rather than to His admonitions, the whole world, having turned the use of steel into more peaceful occupations, would now be living in the most placid tranquility, and would unite in blessed harmony, maintaining inviolate the sanctity of treaties.[37]

24 LACTANTIUS

Lactantius was the last of the prominent apologists prior to the era of Constantine and wrote his massive treatise The *Divine Institutes* about 300 AD. He records also the attitude of the earliest Christians toward military conscription in several sections of his apology.

> For when God forbids us to kill, He not only prohibits us from open violence, which is not even allowed by the public laws, but He warns us against the commission of those things which are esteemed lawful among men. Thus it will be neither lawful for a just man to engage in warfare, since his warfare is justice itself, not to accuse any one of a capital charge, because it makes no difference whether you put a man to death by word, or rather by the sword, since it is the act of putting to death itself which is prohibited.[38] (*Divine Institutes*, Bk. IV, Chap. XX)

> Or why should he carry on war, and mix himself with the passions of others, when his mind is engaged in perpetual peace with men? [The Christian] considers it unlawful not only himself to commit slaughter, but to be

---

[37] Ante-Nicene Fathers, vol. 6, pg. 415
[38] Ante-Nicene Fathers, vol. 7. pg. 187

present with those who do it, and to behold it.[39] (*Divine Institutes*, Bk. V, Chap. XVIII)

In the *Divine Institutes*, Lactantius exposes the errors of pagan religion and the vanity of heather philosophy, and defends the Christian religion and the character of the Christian, which includes conscientious objector to war. Because the Messianic communities were a divine kingdom, enlistment in a military detachment into the service of any nation was alien to their beliefs. The thought of military conscription to wage organized war against another nation labeled as an enemy was repulsive to them.

25 THE DIDIACHE

The Didiache, or Teaching of the Twelve Apostles, is also valuable because it repeats several of the commands of the Sermon on the Mount. The following the introductory chapter.

> THERE are two ways, one of life and one of death; but a great difference between the two ways. The way of life, then, is this: First, thou shalt love God who made thee; second, thy neighbor as thyself; and all things whatsoever thou wouldst should not occur to thee, thou also to another do not do. And of these sayings the teaching is this: Bless them that curse you, and pray for your enemies, and fast for them that persecute you. For what thank is there, if ye love them that love you? Do not also the Gentiles do the same? But do ye love them that hate you; and ye shall not have an enemy. Abstain thou from fleshly and worldly lusts. If one give thee a blow upon thy right cheek, turn to him the other also; and thou shalt be perfect. If one impress thee for one

---

[39] Ante-Nicene Fathers, vol. 7. pg. 153

mile, go with him two. If one take away thy cloak, give him also thy coat. If one take from thee thine own, ask it not back? for indeed thou art not able. Give to every one that asketh thee, and ask it not back; for the Father willeth that to all should be given of our own blessings (free gifts).[40]

26   ATHANASIUS

Athanasius, 298-373 AD, is the transitional prelate from the era of the apologists to the Nicean era, and whose doctrines contained elements of both eras. Anathasius was Bishop of Alexandria 45 years (328-373 AD). He was a fervent opponent of the Arian doctrines, but yet was not tainted by Constantine's reformation of Christianity to meet the needs of the empire. The following are excerpts from *On the Incarnation of the Word*, written about 318 AD.

> 51. The New, Virtue of Continence. Revolution of Society, Purified and Pacified by Christianity:
> 4. For formerly, while in idolatry, Greeks and Barbarians used to war against each other, and were actually cruel to their own kin. For it was impossible for any one to cross sea or land at all, without arming the hand with swords, because of their implacable fighting among themselves. 5. For the whole course of their life was carried on by arms, and the sword with them took the place of a staff, and was their support in every emergency; and still, as I said before, they were serving idols, and offering sacrifices to demons, while for all their idolatrous superstition they could not be reclaimed from this spirit. 6. But when they have come over to the school of Christ, then, strangely enough, as men truly

---

[40] Ante-Nicene Fathers, vol. 7, pg. 377

pricked in conscience, they have laid aside the savagery of their murders and no longer mind the things of war: but all is at peace with them, and from henceforth what makes for friendship is to their liking.

52. Wars, &C., Roused by Demons, Lulled by Christianity.
Who then is He that has done this, or who is He that has united in peace men that hated one another, save the beloved Son of the Father, the common Savior of all, even Jesus Christ, Who by His own love underwent all things for our salvation? For even from of old it was prophesied of the peace He was to usher in, where the Scripture says: "They shall beat their swords into ploughshares, and their pikes into sickles, and nation shall not take the sword against nation, neither shall they learn war any more." 2. And this is at least not incredible, inasmuch as even now those barbarians who have an innate savagery of manners, while they still sacrifice to the idols of their country, are mad against one another, and cannot endure to be a single hour without weapons: 3. but when they hear the teaching of Christ, straightway instead of fighting they turn to husbandry, and instead of arming their hands with weapons they raise them in prayer, and in a word, in place of fighting among themselves, henceforth they arm against the devil and against evil spirits, subduing these by self-restraint and virtue of soul. 4. Now this is at once a proof of the divinity of the Savior, since what men could not learn among idols they have learned from Him; and no small exposure of the weakness and nothingness of demons and idols. For demons, knowing their own weakness, for this reason formerly set men to make war against one another, lest, if they ceased from mutual strife, they should turn to battle against demons. 5. Why, they who become disciples of Christ,

instead of warring with each other, stand arrayed against demons by their habits and their virtuous actions: and they rout them, and mock at their captain the devil; so that in youth they are self-restrained, in temptations endure, in labors persevere, when insulted are patient, when robbed make light of it: and, wonderful as it is, they despise even death and become martyrs of Christ.[41]

The testimony of Athanasius is that barbarian and pagan peoples, having heard the gospel of Jesus Christ, change their mode of life, becoming peaceful and pacifist. Athanasius also mentions that the prophecy of Isaiah 2 is fulfilled in Jesus Christ at the present time.

The following passage is a section of his letter dealing *On Fasting, and Trumpets, and Feasts*, written 329 AD. Athanasius states that the true war is now a spiritual war against sin and temptation, and not a physical war.

3. For the law was admirable, and the shadow was excellent, otherwise, it would not have wrought fear, and induced reverence in those who heard; especially in those who at that time not only heard but saw these things. Now these things were typical, and done as in a shadow. But let us pass on to the meaning, and henceforth leaving the figure at a distance, come to the truth, and look upon the priestly trumpets of our Savior, which cry out, and call us, at one time to war, as the blessed Paul saith, We wrestle not with flesh and blood, but with principalities, with powers, with the rulers of this dark world, with wicked spirits in heaven.[42]

---

[41] Nicene and Post-Nicene Fathers, series 2, vol. 4, pg. 64-65
[42] Nicene and Post-Nicene Fathers, series 2, vol. 4, pg. 507, *Festal Letters*, Letter 1.

This next selection is the letter of Athanasius *To Amun*, written before 354 AD.

> For example, it is not right to kill, yet in war it is lawful and praiseworthy to destroy the enemy; accordingly not only are they who have distinguished themselves in the field held worthy of great honors, but monuments are put up proclaiming their achievements. So that the same act is at one time and under some circumstances unlawful, while under others, and at the right time, it is lawful and permissible.[43]

Athanasius discusses in this passage the hypocrisy of Roman legislature, which prohibits murder on an individual basis, considering it a crime, but approves if it if it is executed on a massive scale by the Roman military.

27   EARLY MARTYRS

Of special testimony to the pacifism of early Christians are the accounts of martyrdom for refusing military service in the Roman army. There are 2 prominent accounts that will be mentioned. The first is Maximilian, who refused service on March 12, 295 AD. In the record of the proceedings, Maximilian, age 21, stated at his induction, "I cannot serve because I am a Christian." He was executed after the hearing.

The second is the martyrdom of Marcellus in 298 AD. He was a centurion in the Roman army and, while in the military, took an oath as a disciple of Jesus and was baptized. Marcellus felt that he could no longer serve in the military and removed the military insignia from himself, along with his sword and belt. Marcellus stated to Agricolanus, a military officer at the trial.

---

[43] Nicene and Post-Nicene Fathers, series 2, vol. 4, pg. 557

"For it is not proper for a Christian, who fears Christ the Lord, to fight for the troubles of this world."

Marcellus was sentenced to death and was executed by decapitation after the trial.

Other martyrs are also mentioned in early accounts, Dasius and Julius for example, who were already soldiers, but then decided to no longer sacrifice to the emperors, meaning, to burn incense while acknowledging his deity.[44]

---

[44] Musurillo, Herbert, *The Acts of Christian Martyrs*, pg 244-279.

PART FOUR

THE DEVELOPMENT OF MILITARIST CHRISTENDOM

And in such a war, it is a Christian act, and an act of love, to kill enemies without scruple, to rob and to burn, and to do whatever damages the enemy, according to the usages of war, until he is defeated. [45]
Martin Luther

28   PLATO AND THE ECUMENICAL FATHERS

What is noticeable in the treatises of the apologists is that many did not advocate the study of OT Bible stories for their students, but rather, the study of Greek philosophy was promoted. The population was entrenched in the various philosophies, including Socrates, Plato, Aristotle, Pythagorus, Plotinus, Epicurus, and Zeno, and the early ecclesiastical apologists felt a knowledge of this was more applicable to the understanding of Christian doctrine rather than a fluency of the OT. Perhaps they feared being branded as Judaizers if they were to emphasize OT Jewish history, law and praises, rather than their own Greek philosophic sages. Clement of Alexandria, for example, felt that Greek philosophy had its origin and derivation from God. He even went to the extreme of stating that Plato was a Greek Moses in his treatise *The Stromata*, Chap. VII.

---

[45] Luther, Martin, *On Secular Authority*

> The Greek preparatory culture, therefore, with philosophy itself, is shown to have come down from God to men.[46]

> And in general terms, we shall not err in alleging that all things necessary and profitable for life came to us from God, and that philosophy more especially was given to the Greeks, as a covenant peculiar to them — being, as it is, a stepping-stone to the philosophy which is according to Christ.[47]

> For what is Plato, but Moses speaking in Attic Greek?[48]

This attitude of Alexander would have led his students to study Plato as a prerequisite to the study of the NT, rather than a study of the OT. Origin in his *Letter to Gregory*, whom he referred to as a son, likewise promoted the study of philosophy as a means of better understanding and interpreting the Bible.

> But I am anxious that you should devote all the strength of your natural good parts to Christianity for your end; and in order to this, I wish to ask you to extract from the philosophy of the Greeks what may serve as a course of study or a preparation for Christianity, and from geometry and astronomy what will serve to explain the sacred Scriptures.[49]

The migration into Christendom of the concepts of Plato regarding his militancy, and the gods of the city-state who justified the edicts of the state, and the concept of the philosopher-king, occurred easily as a result of the study of the

---

[46] Ante-Nicene Fathers, vol. 2, pg. 308
[47] Ante-Nicene Fathers, vol. 2, pg. 495
[48] Ante-Nicene Fathers, vol. 2, pg. 334
[49] Ante-Nicene Fathers, vol. 4, pg. 393

works of Plato by the ecclesiastical apologists and theologians. As far as Augustine was concerned, Plato was more highly valued than the study of the OT. Augustine did not know Hebrew, and knew very little Greek, and was dependant solely on Latin versions of the Bible. In the *City of God*, Augustine lauds Plato:

> But among the disciples of Socrates, Plato was the one who shone with a glory which far excelled that of the others, and who not unjustly eclipsed them all. By birth an Athenian of honorable parentage, he far surpassed his fellow-disciples in natural endowments, of which he was possessed in a wonderful degree.[50]

> If then Plato defined the wise man as one who imitates, knows, loves this God, and who is rendered blessed through fellowship with Him in His own blessedness, why discuss with the other philosophers? It is evident that none come near to us than the Platonists.[51]

The further a student investigates Augustine, the more credible the premise that Augustine plagiarized Plato. Substituting Plato's good with Augustine's God, and Plato's forms with Augustine's triune deity, develops Augustine's theology. The promotion of advocacy of the study of Plato by other ecclesiastical apologists acted as a catalyst for the migration of the concepts of the *Republic* into ecumenical Christendom.

Once Constantine assumed power as philosopher-king, Plato was rebaptized as the new Jesus of the Christendom of Constantine's Roman Empire, as opposed to the Jewish Messiah proclaiming the divine kingdom. As a result of early education in the philosophy of Plato, military service was easily channeled

---

[50] Augustine, *The City of God*, book VIII, chapter 4.
[51] Augustine, book VIII, chapter 5.

into the doctrines of the accepted – and expected – practice of Christians.

29   CONSTANTINE THE GREAT

The history of this era and its prime historical figure is of exceptional importance because of the massive metamorphosis in the Christian Church that occurred as a result of the edicts of Emperor Constantine.

Constantine was a soldier, a general of the Roman army. The turning point in the career of Constantine which was to affect Christianity was his vision at the Milvan Bridge near Rome in 312 AD, during his invasion of Italy to capture Rome, as he was preparing to battle his final competitor Maxentius for sole rule of the Roman Empire. With his army Constantine proceeded into combat and gained the victory over the army of Maxentius his opponent, and took possession of Rome. The following passage is quoted from Eusebius' *Life of Constantine*, Book 1, which was composed as a panegyric for Constantine after his death in 337 AD, (Eusebius died in 340 AD).

> CHAPTER XXVIII: How, while he was praying, God sent him a Vision of a Cross of Light in the Heavens at Midday, with an Inscription admonishing him to conquer by that.
>
> ACCORDINGLY he called on him with earnest prayer and supplications that he would reveal to him who he was, and stretch forth his right hand to help him in his present difficulties. And while he was thus praying with fervent entreaty, a most marvelous sign appeared to him from heaven, the account of which it might have been hard to believe had it been related by any other person. But since the victorious emperor himself long afterwards declared it to the writer of this history, when he was honored with his acquaintance and society, and

confirmed his statement by an oath, who could hesitate to accredit the relation, especially since the testimony of after-time has established its truth? He said that about noon, when the day was already beginning to decline, he saw with his own eyes the trophy of a cross of light in the heavens, above the sun, and bearing the inscription, CONQUER BY THIS. At this sight he himself was struck with amazement, and his whole army also, which followed him on this expedition, and witnessed the miracle.

CHAFFER XXIX: How the Christ of God appeared to him in his Sleep, and commanded him to use in his Wars a Standard made in the Form of the Cross.

He said, moreover, that he doubted within himself what the import of this apparition could be. And while he continued to ponder and reason on its meaning, night suddenly came on ; then in his sleep the Christ of God appeared to him with the same sign which he had seen in the heavens, and commanded him to make a likeness of that sign which he had seen in the heavens, and to use it as a safeguard in all engagements with his enemies.

CHAPTER XXX: The Making of the Standard of the Cross.

AT dawn of day he arose, and communicated the marvel to his friends: and then, calling together the workers in gold and precious stones, he sat in the midst of them, and described to them the figure of the sign he had seen, bidding them represent it in gold and precious stones. And this representation I myself have had an opportunity of seeing.

CHAPTER XXXI: A Description of the Standard of the Cross, which the Romans now call the Labarum.

> Now it was made in the following manner. A long spear, overlaid with gold, formed the figure of the cross by means of a transverse bar laid over it. On the top of the whole was fixed a wreath of gold and precious stones; and within this, the symbol of the Savior's name, two letters indicating the name of Christ by means of its initial characters, the letter P being intersected by X in its center: and these letters the emperor was in the habit of wearing on his helmet at a later period. From the cross-bar of the spear was suspended a cloth, a royal piece, covered with a profuse embroidery of most brilliant precious stones; and which, being also richly interlaced with gold, presented an indescribable degree of beauty to the beholder. This banner was of a square form, and the upright staff, whose lower section was of great length, bore a golden half-length portrait of the pious emperor and his children on its upper part, beneath the trophy of the cross, and immediately above the embroidered banner.
>
> The emperor constantly made use of this sign of salvation as a safeguard against every adverse and hostile power, and commanded that others similar to it should be carried at the head of all his armies.[52]

But what Constantine actually saw in the sky was not a cross, but the Chi-Rho sign, which he placed at the top of his standard as noted above in Chapter XXXI. This is verified by Lactantius, who also records the same event, although not in the same manner as such a brilliant revelation as the record of Eusebius. The following is the record of Lactantius from his treatise *On the Manner in which the Persecutors Died,* Chap. LXIV.

---

[52] Eusebius, *Life of Constantine*, Nicene and Post-Nicene Fathers, series 2, vol. 1. pg. 490-491

Constantine was directed in a dream to cause the heavenly sign to be delineated on the shields of his soldiers, and so to proceed to battle. He did as he had been commanded, and he marked on their shields the letter X, with a perpendicular line drawn through it and turned round thus at the top, being the cipher of CHRIST. Having this sign, his troops stood to arms. The enemies advanced, but without their emperor, and they crossed the bridge. The armies met, and fought with the utmost exertions of valor, and firmly maintained their ground.

The hand of the Lord prevailed, and the forces of Maxentius were routed. He fled towards the broken bridge; but the multitude pressing on him, he was driven headlong into the Tiber.

This destructive war being ended, Constantine was acknowledged as emperor, with great rejoicings, by the senate and people of Rome.[53]

The record of Lactantius is definitely more reliable and accurate than the record of Eusebius for several reasons. Lactantius recorded his within 3 years after the event and as a historical record, while Eusebius' record was part of a panegyric on behalf of Constantine and written 26 years after the fact and after the death of Constantine. What makes Eusebius' account unpalatable is that the command is antithesis to the gospel. At no time did Jesus Christ ever advocate force, much less active armed military force, for any purpose at all. And if the vision would have stated anything at all, it would have repeated the previous commands of the NT in regard to armed struggle: for Constantine to retract and discard his weapon and those of his army, for him to overcome evil with good, to treat his enemy Maxentius with kindness and goodness, to indicate to him that they are not enemies, but could reconcile and live in peaceful

---

[53] Ante-Nicene Fathers, vol. 7, pg. 318.

accord. This author sees a massive disconnect between the account of Eusebius regarding Constantine and the Gospel message. Historian Philip Schaff in his history describes the more probable occurrence, and taken in the light of the more reliable account of Lactantius. Schaff provides the following version of the events:

> But even if we waive the purely critical objections to the Eusebian narrative, the assumed connection, in this case, of the gentle Prince of peace with the god of battle, and the subservience of the sacred symbol of redemption to military ambition, is repugnant to the genius of the gospel and to solid Christian feeling, unless we stretch the theory of divine accommodation to the spirit of the age and the passions and interests of individuals beyond ordinary limits. We should suppose, moreover, that Christ, if he had really appeared to Constantine either in person (according to Eusebius) or through angels, would have exhorted him to repent and be baptized, rather than to construct a military ensign for a bloody battle.[54]

> The facts, therefore, may have been these. Before the battle Constantine, leaning already towards Christianity as probably the best and most hopeful of the various religions, seriously sought in prayer, as he related to Eusebius, the assistance of the God of the Christians, while his heathen antagonist Maxentius, according to Zosimus, was consulting the sibylline books and offering sacrifice to the idols. Filled with mingled fears and hopes about the issue of the conflict, he fell asleep and saw in a dream the sign of the cross of Christ with a significant inscription and promise of victory. Being already familiar with the general use of this sign

---

[54] Schaff, Philip, *History of the Christian Church*, vol. 3, chap. 2.

among the numerous Christians of the empire, many of whom no doubt were in his own army, he constructed the labarum, or rather he changed the heathen labarum into a standard of the Christian cross with the Greek monogram of Christ, which he had also put upon the shields of the soldiers. To this cross-standard, which now took the place of the Roman eagles, he attributed the decisive victory over the heathen Maxentius.[55]

In reality, Constantine's interpretation of his vision and/or dream was opposite to its intent. Jesus was the Prince of Peace, and the purpose of these revelations was to indicate to Constantine that God wanted him to gain control over the empire through reconciliation with his enemy. But since Constantine was a soldier, he proceeded in the manner that he felt proper, that this sign represented a new religion or new deity that would grant him military victory and political control through combat using its emblem. The benefit was mixed: good to Constantine and his concept of Roman government, but detrimental to the original gospel of the spiritual kingdom. As Charles Freeman in his study of the impact of Constantine on philosophy states:

> The adoption of Christianity was not, however to prove entirely straightforward. Constantine knew so little about Christianity that he immediately ran into difficulties. First, Christ was not a God of war. The Old Testament frequently involved God in the slaughter of his enemies, but the New Testament did not. Constantine would have to create a totally new conception of Christianity if he was to sustain the link between the Christian God and the victory in war.[56]

---

[55] Schaff, vol. 3, chap. 2
[56] Freeman, Charles, *The Closing of the Western Mind*, pg. 158.

One of the most important of Constantine's legacies was the creation of a relationship between Christianity and war. Constantine was a brilliant and effective soldier, and he associated his continuing success with the support of the Christian God. Once he had used the victory at the Milvan Bridge as a platform for the granting of toleration to Christians, each new victory strengthened the link.[57]

The benefit of Constantine's effort of giving legal status and freedom to Christianity was mixed: good to Constantine and his concept of Roman government, but detrimental to the original gospel of the Prince of Peace. The bishops of his era traded in their convictions for superficial freedoms, but at the expense of modifying Jesus into a militarist Messiah.

30 THE EFFECTS OF CONSTANTINE

The following year, in January 313 AD, Constantine along with emperor Licinius issued an edict of toleration granting freedom of religion to all residents of the Roman Empire, and which also extended to those calling themselves Christians. This was the famous edict of Milan, and with its issue, persecution against the Christians finally ceased in the Roman Empire. Constantine then proceeded to raise the ecumenical Christian religion, now Christendom, to have the supremacy among all the religions in the Roman Empire. Eusebius mentions this in *The Life of Constantine*, Book 1

> CHAPTER XLII: The Honors conferred upon Bishops, and the Building of Churches.
> The emperor, also personally inviting the society of God's ministers, distinguished them with the highest

---

[57] Freeman, pg. 176.

possible respect and honor, showing them favor in deed and word as persons consecrated to the service of his God. Accordingly, they were admitted to his table, though mean in their attire and outward appearance; yet not so in his estimation, since he thought he saw not the man as seen by the vulgar eye, but the God in him. He made them also his companions in travel, believing that He whose servants they were would thus help him. Besides this, he gave from his own private resources costly benefactions to the churches of God, both enlarging and heightening the sacred edifices, and embellishing the august sanctuaries of the church with abundant offerings.[58]

Christian bishops took advantage of the freedoms that were now extended towards them, and especially after having endured severe persecution just a couple of decades earlier under Diocletian.

Constantine realized the value of having religious harmony in his empire. His reason for issuing an edict of religious toleration was to cease persecution of minority religious groups, and thereby decrease strife within the empire. Christianity valued this as a blessing of God, especially after the persecution under Constantine's predecessor Diocletian. Constantine realized the importance of such an advanced religion and its benefit for his empire, and especially the facets of the teaching that required them to be good citizens and submissive subjects of the emperor. But in time the freedom caused the ecumenical Christian church to evolve into the state-sanctioned religion and intolerance toward those who did not conform to the dictates of the First Ecumenical Council of 325 AD began. As early as 326 AD, Christian denominations that were now labeled heretic or schismatic were excluded from the privileges that Constantine

---

[58] Eusebius, *Life of Constantine*, Nicene and Post-Nicene Fathers, series 2, vol. 1, pg. 494.

conferred on the ecumenical church. Open persecution by the bishops of the ecumenical church followed after, and this especially applied to Christian pacifism denominations. Historian Schaff described it as follows:

> But the elevation of Christianity as the religion of the state presents also an opposite aspect to our contemplation. It involved great risk of degeneracy to the church. The Roman state, with its laws, institutions, and usages, was still deeply rooted in heathenism, and could not be transformed by a magical stroke. The Christianizing of the state amounted therefore in great measure to a paganizing and secularizing of the church. The world overcame the church, as much as the church overcame the world, and the temporal gain of Christianity was in many respects cancelled by spiritual loss. The mass of the Roman empire was baptized only with water, not with the Spirit and fire of the gospel, and it smuggled heathen manners and practices into the sanctuary under a new name.[59]

The religion that Constantine promoted for the empire was not the religion of the Bible. Constantine's concept of a state religion was that of Plato, not Jesus Christ. The resultant religion under the Ecumenical Councils was a Christianity redefined in terms of neo-Platonism. The attempt of the Nicene Fathers working together with the secular authority of the Roman state to create a Christian nation was in reality the materialization of Plato's envisioned *Republic*.

The Christian leaders under Constantine then took the fatal leap of approving this new concept of the gospel. It now became part of Christian service to serve in the Roman military, since the emperor was "Christian" and the empire was "Christian." There was no longer a distinction between the divine and secular

---

[59] Schaff, Philip, *History of the Christian Church*, vol. 3, chap. 13.

kingdoms. This identification of the kingdom of God with the contemporary secular government created in the mind of the population the attitude that service to the government was service to God. To join the military and fight the emperor's battles was to give service to both God and Caesar. The military now under the authority of a "Christian" ruler then promoted the enlistment of Christians and accepted the conversion of soldiers to Christianity. As historian Latourette states:

> Moreover, after the Emperors had espoused Christianity and they and Christian officials were charged with the responsibility for the body politic and for making decisions for the government, the attitude of the majority of Christian towards war changed. Christians now began to believe that some wars are just.[60]

Constantine is heralded by Catholicism and Protestantism as a champion of the cross of Christ, although he continued as a military administrator in his rule over the empire, and permitted the Roman senate to classify him as a god in the tradition of the Roman Emperors. Constantine himself had no personal Christian virtues or morality to speak of; he was a soldier and pagan to his dying day. (He used one of the nails from the cross of Jesus that his mother Helena brought from Jerusalem as a bit for his horse.) It was not until Constantine was on his deathbed that he made confession and was baptized, and even then, by a heretic Arian priest. Constantine is called the Great not because of his morality or ethic, but because he increased the size of his military into a formidable and modern power and was able to expand the size of the Roman Empire into the northern European frontiers and secure them, and reunite the eastern and western divisions into one government under himself.

---

[60] Latourette, K.C., *A History of Christianity*, Vol. 1, pgg. 243-244.

31   AMBROSE

The Roman state worked within the newly legalized and emancipated Christendom to establish militarism as a Christian tenet. However, the problem of how to transform Jesus, the man of peace, into a man of war, persisted.

Ambrose (340–April 4, 397 AD) was governor of northern Italy, with its capital at Milan, and he had a successful career as a lawyer before his career as bishop of Milan, 374 to 397. As a result of his knowledge and experience in Roman government, Ambrose was able to further merge ecumenical Christendom with the Roman state. Ambrose worked close with 5 emperors of the Roman Empire during his 20-year episcopacy: Valentinian I, Gratian, Maximus, Theodosius, and Valentinian II. Ambrose further placed Christendom on the path to accepting military service as part of Christian responsibility toward the state, and primarily the protection of the empire from the invasions of the barbarians. Ambrose equated the Goths with Gog of Ezekiel in one of his treatises, and emphasized that Emperor Gratian had the divine assignment to fulfill the prophetic words and defeat them. The following are selections of *On the Christian Faith*, Book 2, chapter XVI, written about 378 AD.

> 136. I must no further detain your Majesty, in this season of preparation for war, and the achievement of victory Barbarians. Go forth, sheltered, indeed, under the shield of faith, and girt with the sword of the Spirit; go forth to the victory, promised of old time, and foretold in oracles given by God.
>
> 138. That Gog is the Goth, whose coming forth we have already seen, and over whom victory in days to come is promised, according to the word of the Lord: "And they shall spoil them, who had been their despoilers, and plunder them, who had carried off their goods for a prey, saith the Lord. And it shall be in that day, that I will give to Gog"--that is, to the Goths--"a place that is

famous, for Israel an high-heaped tomb of many men, of men who have made their way to the sea, and it shall reach round about, and close the mouth of the valley, and there [the house of Israel shall] overthrow Gog and all his multitude, and it shall be called the valley of the multitude of Gog: and the house of Israel shall overwhelm them, that the land may be cleansed."[61]

In Book 2, chapter XVI of his treatise, *Of the Christian Faith*, Ambrose assured Gratian, "Not military eagles or the flight of birds lead the army, but your name Lord Jesus and Your worship."[62] Ambrose also taught that military defense of a person's country was a Christian virtue, as noted in his *Three Books on the Duties of the Clergy*, Book 1, Chapter XXVII.

> 129. It is clear, then, that these and the remaining virtues are related to one another. For courage, which in war preserves one's country from the barbarians, or at home defends the weak, or comrades from robbers, is full of justice; and to know on what plan to defend and to give help, how to make use of opportunities of time and place, is the part of prudence and moderation, and temperance itself cannot observe due measure without prudence. To know a fit opportunity, and to make return according to what is right, belongs to justice. In all these, too, large-heartedness is necessary, and fortitude of mind, and often of body, so that we may carry out what we wish.[63]

The treatises of Ambrose had a great effect on installing the ecumenical church as the national church of the Roman Empire and endowing it with authority.

---

[61] Nicene and Post-Nicene Fathers, series 2, vol. 10, pg. 22.
[62] Nicene and Post-Nicene Fathers, series 2, vol. 10, pg. 241-242.
[63] Nicene and Post-Nicene Fathers, series 2, vol. 10, pg. 22.

Ambrose also created a greater demarcation between clergy and layperson with his definition of different standards of conduct for each. Since the clergy were busy with the affairs of God, they could not become involved with worldly affairs, which would apply to the common citizen or parishioner. The point to be discussed at the present pertains to war, and this is mentioned by Ambrose in his *Three Books on the Duties of the Clergy*, Book 1, Chapter XXXV (par. 175):

> We have discussed fully enough the nature and force of what is virtuous from the standpoint of justice. Now let us discuss fortitude, which (being a loftier virtue than the rest) is divided into two parts, at home. But the thought of warlike matters seems to be foreign to the duty of our office, for we have our thoughts fixed more on the duty of the soul than on that of the body; nor is it our business to look to arms, but rather to the affairs of peace.[64]

With expositions such at this, the clergy became a sacred caste: laypeople can go to war and kill on their behalf, while clergy will attend to sacramental and sacerdotal duties. In later years, the doctrines of Ambrose – and some of which were already implemented by Emperor Constantine I – led to the exemption of clergy and ministerial students from military service, regardless of their personal convictions or the doctrines of their denomination.

32   BASIL OF CAESAREA

Basil (298-373 AD) was also known as "the Great". He was Bishop of Caesarea (331-379), and was a vehement defender of Nicene doctrines. Basil was one of the Cappadocian Fathers

---

[64] Nicene and Post-Nicene Fathers, series 2, vol. 10, pg. 30.

along with Gregory of Nyssa and Gregory of Nazianzus. The following is *Canon 13*, (part of his letter number 188), written while he was in his episcopal office.

> XIII. Homicide in war is not reckoned by our Fathers as homicide; I presume from their wish to make concession to men fighting on behalf of chastity and true religion. Perhaps, however, it is well to counsel that those whose hands are not clean only abstain from communion for three years.[65]

Basil justifies the Christian vocation of a soldier and warfare, but he also realizes that killing is antithetical to the NT teachings. His only reaction to a Christian having blood on his hands is for him to abstain from communion.

33   AUGUSTINE OF HIPPO

Augustine in his early years was part of the membership of the Manichaeans, who were disciples of Mani. They taught dualism, the ethereal struggle between good and evil forces, and they were also objectors to military service. Augustine became a Manichaean in 373 and was a disciple for 9 years. His letters *Against Faustus*, who was a Manichaean, were written about 400 AD, but Augustine's influence by his mentor Ambrose changed his attitude toward war. Augustine's earlier writings that justified the participation of the Christian in a defensive war seem to treat war in the abstract and subjective, and not as the result of personal experience and conviction, but his new convictions were finally molded as a result of the defeat and sack of Rome by the Goths in 409-410 AD. Augustine now viewed the state and church as 2 divine spheres each having the responsibility to save the nation, including the defense against

---

[65] Nicene and Post-Nicene Fathers, series 2, volume 8.

enemies, and to each of which the Christian had equal obligations. Therefore if the state required war to carry out its purpose, the Christian was required to participate. Augustine's new convictions concurred with the political-religious philosophy of his mentor Ambrose.

As opposed to popular opinion, Augustine did not formulate or compile a just-war theory, although he penned some lines in the *City of God* and other writings on what he felt were sufficient reasons to justify a defense by the state if it was attacked by an aggressive military force – but Christians were not included in the defense. Such justification was not original, but adopted from the Roman philosopher Cicero as well as the Greek Plato. Later generations seem to have taken the little justification available in Augustine and redefined it, attaching his name to something he did not envision, in order to attribute credibility to it. Nonetheless, it becomes apparent after studying *The City of God* that it is Augustine's attempt to justify a defensive war, although he was unable to do so, realizing it was a compromise of principle Christian ethics. Nonetheless, he felt that Christians had an equal responsibility in regard to the security of the state as did non-Christians, and must also contribute their share. The concept of a just-war theory was not developed for another 900 years, first under Thomas Aquinas (to justify the Crusades), and then during the Reformation by Hugo Grotius (to try to curb the religious Thirty Years War of Europe). The basis for the concept of a just-war is Augustine's *City of God*, chapter 19, except that the inclusion of points related to a justifiable war was incidental to the primary topic. Chapter 19 deals with the failure of various philosophers, and philosophy in general, to impose a true peace on earth, and which true peace can only be installed by Christianity. As far as the Roman Empire was concerned, as noted in chapter 7 of the *City of God*, peace is the absence of war, and Augustine condemns war because of its detrimental effect on the population.

> But, say they, the wise man will wage just wars. As if he would not all the rather lament the necessity of just wars, if he remembers that he is a man; for if they were not just he would not wage them, and would therefore be delivered from all wars. For it is the wrongdoing of the opposing party which compels the wise man to wage just wars; and this wrong-doing, even though it gave rise to no war, would still be matter of grief to man because it is man's wrong-doing. Let every one, then, who thinks with pain on all these great evils, so horrible, so ruthless, acknowledge that this is misery. And if any one either endures or thinks of them without mental pain, this is a more miserable plight still, for he thinks himself happy because he has lost human feeling.[66]

As Augustine expounds above, the justification of non-believers – the Roman state – to wage war is that only wise men would initiate a defensive war, and the purpose of such a war would only be defense, defeating the invading enemy to again impose peace. This was in summary the Pax Romana. Augustine's preference is for the wise man to grieve over the necessity of a war, and so preclude it from occurring because of its damage on people and property. Defense in this passage become the sole justifiable purpose to war, and because of war being inherently wrong. An offensive army is wrong to initiate an attack, and the defensive army is likewise in the wrong, because in defending itself it will cause more misery. However, what is notable is that this passage gives greater justification to not defending ourselves in defense if attacked, not to use force as a means of defense, thereby avoiding additional misery and devastation. Remember though, that this passage does not deal with Christians or the Christian church, but a secular state and society in general. Chapter 12 of Book 19 of the *City of God* states:

---

[66] Augustine, *The City of God*, Book 19, chapter 7.

> For even they who make war desire nothing but victory,- -desire, that is to say, to attain to peace with glory. For what else is victory than the conquest of those who resist us? and when this is done there is peace. It is therefore with the desire for peace that wars are waged, even by those who take pleasure in exercising their warlike nature in command and battle. And hence it is obvious that peace is the end sought for by war. For every man seeks peace by waging war, but no man seeks war by making peace. For even they who intentionally interrupt the peace in which they are living have no hatred of peace, but only wish it changed into a peace that suits them better. They do not, therefore, wish to have no peace, but only one more to their mind.[67]

So peace, Augustine writes, means different things to different states. For one state, the absence of war is peace; while for another the conquest of a neighboring state and the institution of a totalitarian rule is peace, like the Pax Romana. This likewise pertains not to Christians, but to pagan and secular states. Chapter 26 of Book 19 mentions temporal peace, which, when applied to the Roman Empire, would be those periods of the absence of war.

Augustine concludes in chapter 28, that war is executed by the wicked of this world, and so it is confined to the secular or earthly city, and not to the city of God. Based on such passages, there is more reason provided in Book 19 for a genuine Christian not to participate in war, and even a defensive war. By not participating in either an offensive or defensive war, the genuine Christian does not identify himself with the temporal peace of the secular earthly city, but with the city of God, which strives after the true divine peace. Augustine realized that only God can introduce true peace on earth, and that wars will also pervade

---

[67] Augustine, *The City of God*, Book 19, chapter 12.

history, since the earthly city will always exist on earth. Nonetheless, Augustine proceeds to provide justification to soldiery, explaining his imbalanced logic, but not in the *City of God*, but in his letter to Faustus, a Manichaean.

> What is the evil in war? Is it the death of some who will soon die in any case, that others may live in peaceful subjection? This is mere cowardly dislike, not any religious feeling. The real evils in war are love of violence, revengeful cruelty, fierce and implacable enmity, wild resistance, and the lust of power, and such like; and it is generally to punish these things, when force is required to inflict the punishment, that, in obedience to God or some lawful authority, good men undertake wars, when they find themselves in such a position as regards the conduct of human affairs, that right conduct requires them to act, or to make others act in this way.[68]

Augustine's conclusion was that since the enemy is going to die at some time anyway in his life, it would be better for him to die the sooner so he would not continue his evil, and that only cowards – referring to religious pacifists – would consider war wrong. If the postulate of Augustine is correct, then it is best to kill the enemy since this will stop him from further perpetrating his crime of killing. But won't each consider the other the aggressor who should be stopped? Each one is doing exactly what the other is doing. And if the enemy is killing another because of orders from his superior, and because of his own conclusion that the war is just, based on his own determination of the war corresponding with the concepts of Augustine's justifiable war, then where is the line of demarcation? Who exactly is the aggressor and who is the defender, since each one claims the same criteria for the justification of their aggression and armed

---

[68] Augustine, *Against Faustus*, 22:74

attack, each one obeying the orders of their respective states? So where is Christian love in this act to kill the attacker, when his criteria for attack are the same? The following paragraph continues his thinking:

> When war is undertaken in obedience to God, who would rebuke, or humble, or crush the pride of man, it must be allowed to be a righteous war; for even the wars which arise from human passion cannot harm the eternal well-being of God, nor even hurt His saints; for in the trial of their patience, and the chastening of their spirit, and in bearing fatherly correction, they are rather benefited than injured. No one can have any power against them but what is given him from above. For there is no power but of God, who either orders or permits. Since, therefore, a righteous man, serving it may be under an ungodly king, may do the duty belonging to his position in the State in fighting by the order of his sovereign,--for in some cases it is plainly the will of God that he should fight, and in others, where this is not so plain, it may be an unrighteous command on the part of the king, while the soldier is innocent, because his position makes obedience a duty,--how much more must the man be blameless who carries on war on the authority of God, of whom every one who serves Him knows that He can never require what is wrong?[69]

In this passage Augustine clearly states that the Christian should fight in a war even if ordered by an ungodly king because of the necessity of obedience to the state, and that he would be innocent of any crime committed, because God requires this obedience to the order of the king.

In the same vein it was very easy for Augustine to rationalize away the statements of Jesus in the Sermon on the Mount:

---

[69] Augustine, *Against Faustus*, 22:75

> If it is supposed that God could not enjoin warfare, because in after times it was said by the Lord Jesus Christ, "I say unto you, That ye resist not evil: but if any one strike thee on the right cheek, turn to him the left also," the answer is, that what is here required is not a bodily action, but an inward disposition.[70]

Based on the above expositions, a Christian soldier should never feel guilty or sense wrong in his actions when killing the enemy on the battlefield when ordered to do so by his commanding officer as long as the soldier has inner inclinations of peace. Therefore, if this conclusion of Augustine is correctly interpreted, external actions must be isolated from personal conviction, and a person could continue to retain Christian humility, but it should not interfere with executing orders. This section also lists a few points that would later become the criteria for a just-war theory:

1. The monarch is to issue the edict for war.
2. The purpose is the peace of the region.
3. Cruelty is not to be utilized, but war is to be waged in love.

Augustine's later letter to Boniface expounds further on his thinking of the justification of defensive war. makes reference to the advice of John the Baptizer and the incident of Jesus and the centurion of Matt 8.

Boniface was a Roman commander defending northern Africa from invaders along the southern borders of the Roman Empire, and he was considering resigning the military because he was now a newly-converted Christian. After seeing what the Goths had done to Rome in 410 AD, Augustine's new Christian soldier had the obligation to preserve the society it was part of by using military defense. Augustine's letter to Boniface in 418 AD

---

[70] Augustine, *Against Faustus*, 22:76

testifies to his convictions. The purpose of Augustine's letter was to convince him that he could remain in his position as a soldier and still be Christian.[71] The justification of Augustine follows in the letter, where he alludes to military figures of the Bible, such as King David, the centurion of Matt 8, and Cornelius, and the advice of John the Baptizer to soldiers. Since the taxes we pay, "to give to Caesar what is Caesar's," are used to pay the wages of soldiers, then, according to Augustine, the vocation of a soldier is acceptable (That the Roman government also used the same taxes to a wide assortment of immorality and vice does not enter into the same argument with Augustine.) The conclusion to Augustine's defense in paragraph 6 is the peace of the Roman Empire as the goal of the Christian soldier, but this advice to Boniface eventually led to Augustine's own suffering and death. About 10 years later, in 427, Boniface revolted against Roman authority. Augustine wrote another letter to Boniface reprimanding him for his revolt against Roman authority, but the admonition was futile. To quell the rebellion, Empress Placidia, wife of Emperor Flavius Constantine II, summoned Goths to northern Africa in 428. Boniface then summoned Vandals as his allies to defend him. But once the Vandals under King Geseric landed in northern Africa, they began an unrestrained devastation of the region, including the siege and defeat of Hippo. Three months into the siege of Hippo, Augustine died.

The primary flaw in the statements of Augustine regarding justifying war is that both sides can claim the same justification. Each side claims that peaceful means of resolution have been exhausted to no success; the war is declared by their sovereign; each nation is defending itself from aggravated assault; each nation is attempting to bring peace by punishing the other for their injustice and atrocity. But war is not war without the death of civilians and the massive destruction of private property.

---

[71] Augustine, *To Boniface*, Letter 189, par. 6.

Augustine's criteria have given Christian denominations greater justification to promoting war, rather than ceasing war.

A contemporary Episcopal priest had the following conclusion in regard to Augustine and the topic of justifiable war:

> I can find no passage in the *City of God* wherein Augustine describes, even theoretically, Christian participation in war, let alone a Christian *obligation* to wage war. To the contrary, he presents the logic of so-called "just-war thinking" as an *inferior and unworthy* logic, a failure on the part of his pagan contemporaries to think through the true nature of human striving for the good. Of the supreme good, which Christians know as the true peace of the City of God, the so-called peace that is trumpeted as the goal of every war is only a dim approximation.[72]

Another major flaw in the rational of Augustine is his direction of specifically focusing on just-war, rather than seeking justification of the violation of any other commandment of God or the Gospel. There are 10 Commandments, and not just the one prohibiting arbitrary killing, and many rules of life that are provided by Jesus Christ and the apostles in the NT, but Augustine seeks no justification to violate any of them, except this one. But could not the same criteria be used towards, for example, adultery? A just-adultery criteria? Or a just-false-witness criteria? Or a just-violate-the-Sabbath criteria? James indicated in his letter, that if a person violates one commandment, he violates them all. Taking Augustine's premises into consideration, the Christian should then be able to utilize the same criteria into justifiably violating every command in the Bible. But this ludicrous approach will never materialize,

---

[72] Elliott, Rev Niel, *Revisiting Augustine & Just-War Theory*

yet it serves to unveil the major flaw of any type of Biblical rational to justify war and military aggression.

34 THOMAS AQUINAS AND CATHOLIC DOCTRINE

Thomas Aquinas was the greatest of theologians of the Catholic church of the Middle Ages, living 1225-1274. He defined Catholic theology for the future generations of Catholics, and is highly respected and very influential at the present in world-wide Catholicism. Thomas Aquinas lived and taught in the era of the 6th, 7th, and 8th Crusades, 1228-1229, 1248-1254, and 1270, respectively. The popes were urging the citizens to war against Islam, whom they labeled as infidels. Three of his brothers were soldiers in the Crusades. The Catholic Church was also waging inquisition and persecution of the Albigences and Bogomils during this same period. His Biblical rational for the justification of war and inquisition was very valuable to the Catholic Church at this time. Thomas Aquinas also taught the legality of slavery and the burning of heretics by the state. Popes Gregory IV and Clement X were in office during the period that Thomas Aquinas was writing his *Summa Theologica* – 1266-1273.

Aquinas' justification for the Crusades was the following:

> It is for this reason that Christ's faithful often wage war with unbelievers, not indeed for the purpose of forcing them to believe, because even if they were to conquer them, and take them prisoners, they should still leave them free to believe, if they will, but in order to prevent them from hindering the faith of Christ. (*Unbelief in General. 8. Whether Unbelievers ought to be Compelled to the Faith?*)[73]

---

[73] Thomas Aquinas, *Summa Theologica*, Part 2 of 2, Question 10.

Thomas Aquinas was also a fervent advocate of capital punishment for heretics, which justification the Popes needed from such a scholar as Thomas Aquinas to justify the inquisition of the Albigences and Bogomils that was in progress.

> I answer that, With regard to heretics two points must be observed: one, on their own side; the other, on the side of the Church. On their own side there is the sin, whereby they deserve not only to be separated from the Church by excommunication, but also to be severed from the world by death. For it is a much graver matter to corrupt the faith which quickens the soul, than to forge money, which supports temporal life. Wherefore if forgers of money and other evil-doers are forthwith condemned to death by the secular authority, much more reason is there for heretics, as soon as they are convicted of heresy, to be not only excommunicated but even put to death. (Heretics. 3. *Whether Heresy ought to be Tolerated?*)[74]

The following section is the justifiable-war theory of Thomas Aquinas, which is based on the original premises provided by Augustine.

> I answer that, In order for a war to be just, three things are necessary. First, the authority of the sovereign by whose command the war is to be waged. For it is not the business of a private individual to declare war, because he can seek for redress of his rights from the tribunal of his superior. Moreover it is not the business of a private individual to summon together the people, which has to be done in wartime. And as the care of the common weal is committed to those who are in authority, it is their business to watch over the common weal of the city,

---

[74] Thomas Aquinas, *Summa Theologica*, Part 2 of 2, Question 11.

kingdom or province subject to them. And just as it is lawful for them to have recourse to the sword in defending that common weal against internal disturbances, when they punish evil-doers, according to the words of the Apostle (Romans 13:4): "He beareth not the sword in vain: for he is God's minister, an avenger to execute wrath upon him that doth evil"; so too, it is their business to have recourse to the sword of war in defending the common weal against external enemies. Hence it is said to those who are in authority (Psalm 81:4): "Rescue the poor: and deliver the needy out of the hand of the sinner"; and for this reason Augustine says (*Against Fautus*, xxii, 75): "The natural order conducive to peace among mortals demands that the power to declare and counsel war should be in the hands of those who hold the supreme authority."

Secondly, a just cause is required, namely that those who are attacked, should be attacked because they deserve it on account of some fault. Wherefore Augustine says: A just war is wont to be described as one that avenges wrongs, when a nation or state has to be punished, for refusing to make amends for the wrongs inflicted by its subjects, or to restore what it has seized unjustly.

Thirdly, it is necessary that the belligerents should have a rightful intention, so that they intend the advancement of good, or the avoidance of evil. Hence Augustine says (*De Verb. Dom.*) "True religion looks upon as peaceful those wars that are waged not for motives of aggrandizement, or cruelty, but with the object of securing peace, of punishing evil-doers, and of uplifting the good." For it may happen that the war is declared by the legitimate authority, and for a just cause, and yet be rendered unlawful through a wicked intention. Hence Augustine says (*Against Faustus,* xxii, 74): The passion for inflicting harm, the cruel thirst for vengeance, an unpacific and relentless spirit, the fever of revolt, the lust of power, and such like things, all these are rightly condemned in war.[75]

As mentioned above, Aquinas specified 3 conditions for a just war in his *Summa Theologica*: 1. The ruler under whom the war is to be fought must have authority to do so. 2. A just cause is required. 3. The war has as its purpose a right intention: to achieve some good or avoid some evil. Much like Augustine's criteria for a just war, Aquinas' criteria likewise gave Christians greater justification for waging war than ceasing it. Thomas Aquinas confirmed Augustine's just war criteria as valid Catholic doctrine, but not without good reason.

> But in matters concerning the disposal of actions and human affairs, a subject is bound to obey his superior within the sphere of his authority; for instance a soldier must obey his general in matters relating to war, a servant his master in matters touching the execution of the duties of his service, a son his father in matters relating to the conduct of his life and the care of the household; and so forth.[76]
> Now the order of justice requires that subjects obey their superiors, else the stability of human affairs would cease. Hence faith in Christ does not excuse the faithful from the obligation of obeying secular princes.[77]

The above statements on the obedience of the Christian to secular authorities are a parallel of Augustine on the same topic. Therefore, based on the conclusions of Thomas Aquinas, any disregard or defiance against any order of the state can be easily

---

[75] Thomas Aquinas, *Summa Theologica*, Part 2 of 2, Question 40: War. 1. Whether it is always Sinful to Wage War.
[76] Thomas Aquinas, Question 104: Obedience. 5. Whether Subjects are Bound to Obey their Superiors in all Things.
[77] Thomas Aquinas. Obedience. 6. *Whether Christians are Bound to Obey the Secular Powers.*

construed as a disregard or defiance of the command God Himself, as the state interprets the command of God.

The Catechism of the Catholic Church of 1994 in Section 2309, *Avoiding War,* provides the following as the present official doctrine regarding war. [78]

> The strict conditions for legitimate defense by military force require rigorous consideration. The gravity of such a decision makes it subject to rigorous conditions of moral legitimacy. At one and the same time:
> > The damage inflicted by the aggressor on the nation or community of nations must be lasting, grave, and certain;
> >
> > All other means of putting an end to it must have been shown to be impractical or ineffective;
> >
> > There must be serious prospects of success;
> >
> > The use of arms must not produce evils and disorders graver than the evil to be eliminated. The power of modern means of destruction weighs very heavily in evaluating this condition
>
> These are the traditional elements enumerated in what is call the "Just-War" doctrine. The evaluation of these conditions for moral legitimacy belongs to the prudential judgment of those who have responsibility for the common good. [79]

As mentioned above on the section on Augustine, war is not war without the massive destruction of the enemy's armed forces, country and population, and such criteria as above then becomes unrealistic, since wars are waged to be won by whatever means is necessary, and not to be lost. The section also deals solely with "defensive war." In no place in the Catholic Catechism is there any mention of proceeding with an "offensive" war, or attacking

---

[78] This edition carries the imprimatur of Joseph Cardinal Ratzinger, the former Pope Benedict XVI.
[79] *Catechism of the Catholic Church*, Liguori Publications, pg. 555-556.

a neutral or unpretentious nation. Yet, the Catholic Church historically has supported every state that it has been located in with any war that the state decides to wage, whether defensive or offensive.

35   MARTIN LUTHER

With the dissolution of the authority of both Western Catholicism and Eastern Orthodoxy during the middle ages, a number of smaller denominations were created. Each had their own founder with a specific set of religious criteria for their denomination. The majority of these incorporated the concepts of Augustine regarding military service and his just war theory into their confession of faith, while a few held to conscientious objection. Both classes of militant and pacifist churches will be discussed.

Luther viewed the state as the civil arm of God, which became the dominant trend of thought in Protestantism. He believed that government was installed by God and which proceeded to govern the state as the supreme authority. Luther had the view that the state governed by divine providence, and so the citizens had the obligation of obedience to the state in the manner the state understood the will of God. This then proceeds to the question of war in the thinking of Luther. He taught that the soldier was the servant of the state, and that the state ruling by divine providence is allegorically given the sword by God to fulfill His will as the state sees fit. Luther described it in this manner.

> Since your whole country is placed in danger [by war], you must consider whether God will help you, so that everything does not go to wrack and ruin; and even if you cannot help making some widows and some orphans, you must at least prevent total ruin, and nothing but widows and orphans [being left]. The

subjects for their part owe obedience and must set their lives and goods to it. For in such a case everyone must risk his goods and even himself, for the sake of his neighbor. And in such a war, it is a Christian act, and an act of love, to kill enemies without scruple, to rob and to burn, and to do whatever damages the enemy, according to the usages of war, until he is defeated. But beware of sins and of violating women and maidens. And when the enemy is defeated, then those who surrender and submit are to be shown mercy and granted peace. In other words, act according to the maxim 'God helps the strongest.' Abraham did so when he defeated the four kings. Of course, he killed many and did not show much mercy until the victory was his. A case like this should be regarded as something sent by God, so that for once the land is swept clean of villains. But what if a prince is in the wrong? Are his people obliged to obey him even then? No, because no one has a duty to act unjustly; we must obey God (who will have justice prevail), rather than men.[80]

Luther in this manner hoped to reassure the Christians who were in the military that their service to the state in combat was acceptable and proper service to God. Luther continued the theology of the post-Nicene Fathers, having abolished the distinction between the divine and secular by stating that service to the state is service to God. Luther's attitude toward Jews however was inherently malicious.

Accordingly, it must and dare not be considered a trifling matter but a most serious one to seek counsel against this and to save our souls from the Jews, that is, from the devil and from eternal death. My advice, as I said earlier, is:

---

[80] Luther, Martin, *On Secular Authority*

First, that their synagogues be burned down, and that all who are able toss in sulphur and pitch; it would be good if someone could also throw in some hell fire. That would demonstrate to God our serious resolve and be evidence to all the world that it was in ignorance that we tolerated such houses, in which the Jews have reviled God, our dear Creator and Father, and his Son most shamefully up till now, but that we have now given them their due reward.[81]

Luther's rabid advice for the Christian attitude toward the Jews did him no benefit at all, and did his followers no benefit, as they put his words into practice. The passage allows the reader to sense the departure of the reformers from the example of the apostles toward unrepentant Jews: first Stephan, while being stoned to his death, said, Lord do not hold this sin against them. Acts 7:59. While Jesus said for the disciples to shake the dust off their feet and continue on their way if a city rejects his gospel.

The Peasants War of 1524-1525 evolved from the thinking that peasants developed, that the teachings of Martin Luther would affect the social and economic system as well as the ecclesiastical. Revolts of peasants broke out in several German states against the feudal and aristocratic princes, which turned into an all-out civil war. The peasant rebels destroyed palaces, castles, convents, and libraries, and executed priests and landlords. Initially, Luther had sympathy with the cause of the peasant rebels, that many of their grievances were legitimate and genuine, and he condemned the oppressive practices of the aristocracy, but as the devastation continued, Luther turned against the revolt. Much of Luther's stance toward the peasantry was political: he was first the child of peasants, but in his present condition, he was dependant on the German princes and their political support was important for him to continue his

---

[81] Luther, Martin, *On the Jews and their Lies*, chapter 17.

work of ecclesiastical reformation. Luther could not risk estranging himself from those who protected and supported him. As Luther wrote in a letter dated May 30, 1525 to Nicholas Ansdorf at Magdeburg:

> My opinion is that it is better that all the peasants be killed than that the princes and magistrates perish, because the rustics took the sword without divine authority. The only possible consequence of their satanic wickedness would be the diabolic devastation of the kingdom of God. Even if the princes abuse their power, yet they have it of God, and under their rule the kingdom of God at least has a chance to exist. Wherefore no pity, no tolerance should be shown to the peasants, but the fury and wrath of God should be visited upon those men who did not heed warning nor yield when just terms were offered them, but continued with satanic fury to confound everything... To justify, pity, or favor them is to deny, blaspheme, and try to pull God from heaven.[82]

By the time the armies of the feudal princes and aristocrats suppressed the revolt, about 100,000 peasants had been killed in battle. Luther's abandonment of the cause of the peasants – their social and economic despair – and his alliance with Germany's rich and powerful, alienated the peasants from him and his gospel. The presence of Lutheranism became meager in the areas affected by the Peasants War and the Catholic counter-reformation made great strides in these regions.

The gospel that Martin Luther taught may have been fine for the middle classes, artisans, free citizens, feudal princes and aristocrats, but it was a gospel pertaining to a reformation of ecclesiasticism and sacerdotalism, which meant little to the masses of German serfs and peasants and did nothing for their

---

[82] Smith, Preserved, *The life and Letters of Martin Luther*, pg. 164-165

social and economic despair. Rather than exerting the effort for reconciliation of the 2 parties – peasants and aristocrats – and instituting economical equity or better social and working conditions for the peasants, Luther urged the violent suppression of the peasants, which he felt he had to do, so not to lose the support of the wealthy and powerful whom he needed for his reformation.

36   JOHN CALVIN

Calvinism was largely grounded in the reformation of Luther and used many of the same arguments to approve of military service and the relationship between church and state. Calvin was far more militant than Luther, teaching that the church and state were to work together in one loyal alliance for a common goal.

Calvin felt that the state was subject to the church, following the concept of Israel in the Old Testament, thus creating a "Christian state" in Protestantism. Calvin felt he solved the problem of the conflict between the secular and spiritual by having the state subject itself to Christian law, but a Christian law based on the Old Testament concept of a theocracy and not on the concept of the divine kingdom of the New Testament. This included the execution of heretics.

Calvin had no difficulty in providing an acceptable place for military conscription in his Christian state, using all the arguments and justifications of the Old Testament. The areas dealing with pacifism in the New Testament were rewritten and interpreted out of recognition by Calvin. He himself advocated and participated in the defense of his new Christian denomination using military force. The following are the 2 passages in the *Institutes* that deal with the subject.

> As it is sometimes necessary for kings and states to take up arms in order to execute public vengeance, the reason assigned furnishes us with the means of estimating how

far the wars which are thus undertaken are lawful. For if power has been given them to maintain the tranquility of their subjects, repress the seditious movements of the turbulent, assist those who are violently oppressed, can they rise it more opportunely than in repressing the fury of him who disturbs both the ease of individuals and the common tranquility of all; who excites seditious tumult, and perpetrates acts of violent oppression and gross wrongs? If it becomes them to be the guardians and maintainers of the laws, they must repress the attempts of all alike by whose criminal conduct the discipline of the laws is impaired. Nay, if they justly punish those robbers whose injuries have been inflicted only on a few, will they allow the whole country to be robbed and devastated with impunity? Since it makes no difference whether it is by a king or by the lowest of the people that a hostile and devastating inroad is made into a district over which they have no authority, all alike are to be regarded and punished as robbers. Natural equity and duty, therefore, demand that princes be armed not only to repress private crimes by judicial inflictions, but to defend the subjects committed to their guardianship whenever they are hostilely assailed. Such even the Holy Spirit, in many passages of Scripture, declares to be lawful.[83]

But if it is objected that in the New Testament there is no passage or example teaching that war is lawful for Christians, I answer, first, that the reason for carrying on war, which anciently existed, still exists in the present day, and that, on the other hand, there is no ground for debarring, magistrates from the defense of those under them; And, secondly, that in the Apostolical writings we are not to look for a distinct exposition of

---

[83] Calvin, Jean, *Institutes of the Christian Religion*, Book 4; chapter 20, section 11.

those matters, their object being not to form a civil polity but to establish the spiritual kingdom of Christ; lastly, that there also it is indicated, in passing, that our Savior, by his advent, made no change in this respect. For (to use the words of Augustine) "if Christian discipline condemned all wars, when the soldiers asked counsel as to the way of salvation, they would have been told to cast away their arms, and withdraw altogether from military service. Whereas it was said, (Luke 3: 14,) Concuss no one, do injury to no one, be contented with your pay. Those who he orders to be contented with their pay he certainly does not forbid to serve,"[84]

Calvin's ecclesiastical polity was a theocracy, with the rule of the word of God as interpreted by Calvin as the law of the state. His arguments for a NT theocracy however were based on the OT, and the state would support the official church of the state. Just as with Augustine, Calvin viewed the advice of John the Baptizer as justification for the vocation of a soldier, even though John was the last of the OT prophets.

Following the laws for the punishment of criminals in the OT, Calvin did not hesitate to order the execution of a child for discrediting her mother, another child for striking her parents, an adulterer, a woman accused of witchcraft, and one person for atheism. The most infamous of Calvin's prosecutions was the anti-Trinitarian Michael Servetus, who was executed on October 27, 1553. Calvin felt the Christian magistrate had the right and duty to punish heresy by death. Heresy, of course, was defined by Calvin.

---

[84] Calvin, Jean, *Institutes of the Christian Religion*, Book 4; chapter 20, section 12.

37 THE FRUITS OF REFORMATION THEOLOGY AND HUGO GROTIUS

The theology produced by the later theologians, both Catholic and Protestant, circumvented the pacifism of the early church and succumbed to the concepts of Thomas Aquinas and his peers due to pressure from popes and kings of Europe during the middle ages. As much error that the reformers were able to rectify during their era, they were still unable to return to the apostolic concepts of the Prince of Peace and so continued the approval of military service.

The Thirty-Years War was the direct result of the theology of Calvin and Luther in actual practice. This war was actually a series of religious wars between the 2 main Protestants divisions – Luther and Calvin – and the Catholics in Europe, 1618-1648, and dealt with which religion would possess the political and military hegemony in Europe. The fruits of Protestant theology was the military devastation of Europe and increased enmity between Catholicism and Protestantism.

Hugo Grotius was a political philosopher of the early 17th century, who further developed the concept of a just-war theory and completed it in its present form. Grotius' purpose, however, was not the same as that of the ecclesiastical fathers in their development of a just-war theory. Grotius hoped to utilize the theory as an attempt to curb the vast amount of war that Christian churches had been involved in, beginning with the several Crusades, and now in the midst of the 30-year long religious war, by providing them with patristic evidence proving that their denominational conflicts did not meet any of the criteria for a just-war. Grotius sincerely expected the 3 primary Christian denominations – Catholic, Lutheran and Calvinist – to seriously consider the prerequisites for a war to be justifiable, and then desist. This attempt only back-fired on Grotius and he was arrested by Calvinists in 1618 and sentenced to life in prison without charges being filed against him. He escaped from his prison after 3 years confinement. Grotius wrote his treatise *On the Law of War and Peace* in 1625.

> I saw in the whole Christian world a license of fighting at which even barbarous nations might blush. Wars were begun on trifling pretexts or none at all, and carried on without any reference of law, Divine or human.[85]

> IV. It admits of some doubt, whether those, who unintentionally obstruct our defense, or escape, which are necessary to our preservation, may be lawfully maimed or killed. There are some, even Theologians, who think they may. And, certainly if we look to the law of nature alone, according to its principles, our own preservation should have much more weight with us, than the welfare of society. But the law of charity, especially the evangelical law, which has put our neighbor upon a level with ourselves, does not permit it.[86]

In 1635, Grotius was able to assist the diplomats of various countries and Christian leaders to negotiate a treaty to end the Thirty Years War. Grotius, with all his effort to curb war – and especially the conflicts between the denominations attempting to gain the hegemony in Europe – was unable to achieve his goal, as Christian denominations in later years utilized his work as a means to justify Christian militarism rather than curb it.

---

[85] Grotius, Hugo, *On the Law of War and Peace*, Prolegomena
[86] Grotius, Hugo, *On the Law of War and Peace*, book 2, chap. 1

PART FIVE

HISTORY OF CHRISTIAN PACIFISM

Since the time that Jesus Christ said, Put up thy sword into its sheath, Christians ought not to go to war.
Desiderius Erasmus

38 THE MONTANISTS

The extant history of small Christian denominations and sects that separated from the doctrine of the ecumenical church during the early centuries is very brief and meager. However there is sufficient evidence to establish a continuous vein of thinking from the ante-Nicene era to the present pertaining to conscientious objection as part of the gospel of the divine kingdom.

The Montanists of central Turkey of the 2nd to the 5th centuries were most likely pacifist. The group at its initiation would have had close ties to the original disciples of the apostles, and their refusal to be part of the Roman military coincided with their eschatological convictions. This conclusion is also based on the available information of Tertullian who was a Montanist for several years.

39   MANI AND MANICHAEISM

Mani is included in this history as a result of his incorporation of some unadulterated teachings of Jesus Christ into his eclectic religion. Mani was born with the Persian name Shuriak about 216 AD. At the age of about 20 he had a vision and, inspired by divine revelation, he proceeded as a new prophet, called himself an Apostle of Jesus Christ, and proclaimed himself to be Mani, meaning, the Vessel. Mani's teaching is a synthesis of the teachings of Zoroaster, Buddha and Jesus Christ, and had a very high morality and ethic.

> The vast bulk of Mani's adherents -- ninety-nine out of every hundred -- were Hearers. They were bound by Mani's Ten Commandments only, which forbade idolatry, mendacity, avarice, murder (i.e. all killing), fornication, theft, seduction to deceit, magic, hypocrisy, secret infidelity (to Manichaeism).[87]

Mani taught Christian pacifism, and his religion persevered for several centuries throughout the Mediterranean world. Augustine's letter against the Manicheans includes his section refuting them for refusing to engage in war or military service.

40   MARCION

Marcion was the son of a bishop of Sinope, a city in the north-central region of present-day Turkey along the Black Sea. After being educated and instructed as a priest, he was attracted to Gnosticism. Rejecting the OT, Marcion reformulated the books of the NT to suit his conviction. He rejected the cruel Jehovah of the OT in favor of the God of love of the NT, who revealed himself in Jesus Christ. Dualism was likewise part of Marcion's

---

[87] Arendzen, J.P., *Mani and His Message*

theology: suppression of the body through ascetic practices to increase the spiritual aspects of the Christian life. Marcion taught a high standard of morality and ethic, imposing self-discipline, and forbidding the consumption of meat and alcohol. As a result, Marcion included non-violence into his doctrines (just as did Mani, also a dualist). The idea of participation in war and violence was repulsive to Marcion, and was antithetical to his view of the God of the NT, who was kind, forgiving, and full of love.

Schaff quotes a passage of Marcion from his book *Antithesis*:

> The God of the Old Testament is harsh, severe and unmerciful in His law. He commands, Love you neighbor, but hate your enemies, and return an eye for an eye and a tooth for a tooth. But the God of the New Testament commands, Love your enemies.[88]

Harnack in his book *Militia Christi* states that according to the teachings of Marcion, the Father of Jesus Christ "was gracious, compassionate, brought peace and forbade striving and war," and that Marcion understood the Christian concept of God in an essentially correct way.[89]

Marcion's followers of later centuries influenced the Paulicians and Cathari, who held similar doctrines.

41 PAULICIANS

Paul of Samosota is traditionally the founder of the sect that bears his name, the Paulicians, although others claim that the honor belongs to Apostle Paul, whose writings were highly respected and observed. Paul of Samosota was a bishop of Antioch during the 3rd quarter of the 3rd century AD. His

---

[88] Schaff, Philip, *History of the Christian Church*, vol 2, chapter 127.
[89] Harnack, Adolf, *Militia Christi*, pg. 46

disciples were primarily living in central and eastern Turkey and Armenia. The Paulicians absorbed several of the tenets of Marcion (hence their respect for Apostle Paul): they were dualist, believing that matter was created by the cruel and imperfect Jehovah of the OT. Paulicians were iconoclastic and rejected all the rites of the ecumenical church and all material symbols used in ecclesiastical worship. The only rite they observed was baptism at the age of 30, following the example of Jesus Christ. The Paulicians were likewise pacifist, as Steven Runciman mentions in his history regarding them.

> The authorities in that hard bellicose age, with civilization on the defensive against the barbarian invader, could not approve of a faith wherein all killing, even of animals, was forbidden, and whereof a considerable number of believers wandered about, refusing to work, refusing to notice secular regulations, and exercising a vast influence on the whole community...[90]

Under Emperor Justinian in the 6th century, some 100,000 were executed by order of his wife Theodora, and the balance were exiled to the Balkans. There in the following centuries many compromised their tenets and joined the Roman military to escape further persecution. The influence of the Paulicians migrating east into Bulgaria to escape persecution gave impetus to the rise of another sect, the Bogomils.

42   BOGOMILES

The Bulgarian Bogomils, 'The Friends of God," were also known as Patarines and Messalians. They were earnest and ascetic, having acquired their tenets from the earlier Paulicians that

---

[90] Runciman, Steven, *The Medieval Manichee*, pg. 17

were exiled to the Balkans, and whose influence then spread east into Bulgaria.. They primarily lived in Bulgaria, and likewise repudiated the Catholic rites and theology and were pacifist. They flourished during the 8th through the 12th centuries. Runciman likewise states regarding them:

> But the true Bogomils were unwilling to shed blood.[91]

With the beginning of the Crusades, they steadily migrated further east into Russia, and there in later centuries influenced the individuals who formed the sects of the Strigolniki and Judaizers. Bogomils of the 12th century had lost by that time their dualist philosophy and were closer to the contemporary Baptists in doctrine and practice.

43   THE CATHARI AND ALBIGENCES

The Cathari were the popular name of the group, which was derived from the Greek kathros, meaning pure. In southern France they were known as the Albigences from the city Albi, one of their capitals. This group appeared in historical records about the year 1000 AD, with the appearance of members who rejected the rites and teachings of the Catholic church. They continued the tenets of the Paulicians and assimilated many of the doctrines of the Bogomils. This group re-introduced pacifism into the instruction and practice of those seeking a true teaching of the gospels, as opposed to that of the Catholic church. Historians Philip Schaff and Latourette describes them as follows:

> The condemnation of capital punishment was based on such passages as, Give place unto wrath, vengeance is Mine, I will repay, saith the Lord, Rom 12:19; and the

---

[91] Runciman, pg. 68

judicial execution of heretics and criminals was pronounced homicide, a survival from the Old Testament and the influence of its evil god. The Cathari quoted Christ's words, You have heard bow it has been said, An eye for an eye and a tooth for a tooth. One of the charges made against the established church was that is countenanced war and marshaled armies.[92]

Cathari were not to engage in war.[93]

The Cathari reached the apex of their numbers at the beginning of the 12th century, numbering about 4 million. Eventually, massive persecution by the Catholic church beginning in 1120 AD, broke the sect and caused them to assimilate into the general population. The Inquisition under Pope Innocent III especially affected the Albigences and Waldenses.

44 PIERRE WALDES AND THE WALDENSES

He was also known as Peter Waldo, founder of the Christian sect that became known as the Waldenses. Pierre Waldes lived in Lyons, France toward the end of the 12th century, about 100 years before Thomas Aquinas, and during the 2nd and 3rd Crusades. Unlike the Cathari and Bogomils, the Waldenses attempted to work within the Catholic and reform it, much like the earlier disciples of Martin Luther. However, as a result of their preaching, the Waldenses were excommunicated by the pope in 1184 at the Council of Verona, and then they were treated as heretics. They were then included in the inquisition of the 14th century against the Albigenses, and the Piedmont Waldenses suffered the most in the Catholic persecution of the 15th century. One Baptist historian concluded the following:

---

[92] Schaff, Philip, *History of the Christian Church*, vol 5, chapter 80.
[93] Latourette, K.C., *A History of Christianity*, Vol. 1, pg. 454.

> The very charges against them, in reference to personal revelations and the community of good, or opposition to war and oaths, to which the apostolic and modern communities are equally liable, only more clearly attest their exalted life, character, and discipline.[94]

The Waldenses were pacifist, and accepted the New Testament literally. The group spread from southern France to Italy and then into Germany. In Italy, they were known as the Lombards. The sect lasted into the era of the Protestant reformation and then apparently assimilated into other denominations, and primarily the Reformed Faith.

45 PETER CHELCHEKY AND THE CZECH BRETHREN

He was also known as Peter of Chelcice, or Chelchitzki, living about 1390-1460. He was originally a disciple of John Huss, a Czech Christian reformer who was burned at the stake as a heretic by the Catholic church in 1415. His group became known as the Bohemian or Czech Brethren. His group adhered to a literal interpretation of the New Testament and was pacifist. The Czech Brethren lasted as a denomination until the 1620's when the majority joined local Protestant sects and abandoned their earlier precepts. Peter wrote the following remonstrance against ecumenical Christendom and its advocates of militarism:

> The whole rabble of these divided multitudes are called Christians and together they pray: Our Father which art in heaven. They approach God in this way while each party has in mind the destruction of the other. They think they are serving God by shedding others' blood. And on both sides they say: Forgive us as we forgive.

---

[94] Everts, W.W., *The Church in the Wilderness, or, the Baptists before the Reformation*

And every party seeks to increase its military force and never thinks of forgiving the other so long as they can hope to overcome them. Therefore their prayers are blasphemies against God.[95]

Peter's rage is directed at the fact that soldiers on both sides of armed warfare call themselves Christians, and pray to God to give them the victory over their opponents, indicative of hypocrisy.

46   DESIDERIUS ERASMUS

Erasmus lived about 1460 to 1535, in France and Switzerland. He was not a religious Christian but was a humanist, believing that the way to truth was through scholarship. His claim to prominence in Christian history was his publication of the Greek New Testament and other books of the early apologists. He especially taught that war and military service were incompatible with the teachings of Christ. As Erasmus wrote:

> They who defend war must defend the dispositions which lead to war, and these dispositions are absolutely forbidden by the gospel. Since the time that Jesus Christ said, Put up thy sword into its sheath, Christians ought not to go to war. Christ suffered Peter to fall into an error in this matter, on purpose that, when he had put up Peter's sword, it might remain no longer a doubt that war was prohibited, which before that order had been considered as allowable.[96]

---

[95] E. Egli, *Die Zuercher Wiedertaeufer zur Reformationszeit*, (quoted from *The Principle of Nonresistance*, John Horsch)
[96] quoted from *An Inquiry into the Accordancy of War*, Jonathan Dymond, pg. 36.

Indirectly, Erasmus was a catalyst to the reformation movement, even though there occurred many conflicts between him and Martin Luther and other reformers.

47 MENNO SIMONS AND THE MENNONITES

Menno Simons was a ex-Catholic Franciscan priest who lived in the Netherlands, about 1496 to 1561. He became a priest in 1524 but abandoned the Catholic church and priesthood about 1534 after a personal study of the Bible. He joined the Anabaptist movement and later became a leader of a group in Holland and north-west Germany. They became known as the Mennonites.

One of the main precepts of Menno Simons was conscientious objection to military service. His group was persecuted for this in later years. The Mennonite congregations increased in Germany and eastern Europe in subsequent generations, but became a wandering sect for a while, journeying to escape persecution. Many immigrated to Russia, and later many immigrated to America. The Mennonites in America have been a tremendous promoter of the attitude of conscientious objection and have offices available for support and consultation for those who seek assistance in avoiding military service.

> A strong Mennonite belief is nonviolence or pacifism. Mennonites believe that violence is never the best answer to problems or conflict, and that Jesus taught us a better way than the way of fighting and wars. They try to take seriously Jesus' words to love your enemy. For that reason, Mennonites do not take part in war. During World War II, many Mennonites in the United States served in Civilian Public Service rather than participate in fighting. Some Mennonites chose to serve in non-combatant positions. Still others refused to register at all. Some Mennonites today choose not to pay the

portion of their taxes that goes to maintaining the military.[97]

The following is a selection from the writings of Menno Simons:

> The regenerated do not go to war, nor engage in strife. They are the children of peace who have beaten their swords into plowshares and their spears into pruning hooks, and know of no war. They render unto Caesar the things that are Caesar's and unto God the things that are God's. Their sword is the sword of the Spirit which they wield with a good conscience through the Holy Ghost.[98]

During World War 1, 138 Mennonites were courts-martialed and sentenced to incarceration for refusing induction into the armed forces. During World War 2, 4,665 Mennonites were COs (conscientious objectors) and assigned to civilian public service, while about 1,200 were absolutists and incarcerated at various prisons, During the Vietnam War, Mennonites provided 8,000 COs in 1968, 8,800 COs in 1969, and 11,000 COs in 1970.

48   JACOB HUTTER AND THE HUTTERITES

A group of German Anabaptists who migrated to Moravia in southeast Europe under Jacob Hutter in the 1530's became known as the Hutterites. They were driven into exile similar to their Dutch cousins the Mennonites due to religious persecution. Non-violence was a firm part of their religious persuasion. Additional persecution in later years forced the Hutterites to move to the Ukraine in the 1770's, and then into Russia in 1802, seeking religious freedom and the ability to live as conscientious

---

[97] Who Are the Mennonites?
[98] Simons, Menno, *Complete Works*, Part II, pg. 170b.

objectors. Many Hutterites then migrated from Russia to America and Canada after Tsar Alexander II passed the universal military service act of 1874.

The following is a selection from the writings of Jacob Hutter:

> We will not do a wrong or an injury to any man, yea, not to our greatest enemy, neither to Ferdinandus,[99] nor any one else, great or small. All our actions and conduct, word and work, life and walk, are open; there is no secret about it all. Rather than knowingly to rob a man of a penny we would willingly give up a hundred guilders. And before we would give our greatest enemy a blow with the hand, to say nothing of spear, sword or halberd as is the manner of the world, we would be willing to lose our lives.[100]

The difficulties for Hutterites was increased beyond that of simple persecution for refusal of conscription. Their German language, custom and traditions caused war hysteria patriots during WW1 to be very suspicious of them and to identify them with the Germany that American was at war with. In public schools of fourteen states of the USA, the use of the German language was prohibited.

> Before World War I most Hutterite communities were located in South Dakota. During the war, however, there was widespread popular disapproval of the Hutterites based on a combination of factors. Their use of the German language and their insistence on the use of German for religious instruction was one problem. Their refusal to serve in the military or to support the war in other ways, such as by purchasing war bonds, was

---

[99] Holy Roman Emperor, 1558-1564.
[100] quoted from John Horsh, *The Principle of Nonresistance as held by the Mennonite Church, 1985.*

another problem. Added to this was a fear and mistrust of a people who purchased large tracts of land but kept to themselves and wanted to have as little to do as possible with neighboring non-Hutterite communities. Distrust of the Hutterites in South Dakota reached the point that there were state laws passed to restrict their influence and set limits on their acquisition of land. Beginning in 1918, many of the Hutterite communities in South Dakota disposed of their property there and moved to Canada.

Like other Anabaptists, the Hutterites are conscientious objectors opposed to any kind of military service. At the time of World War I some of them received shocking mistreatment from the authorities because of their refusal to be inducted into the army or to wear uniforms.[101]

Few Hutterite communities remain in America at present as a result of the religious persecution they suffered in America during the world wars.

49 GEORGE FOX AND THE QUAKERS (SOCIETY OF FRIENDS)

George Fox is rightly called the founder of the Quakers, today known as the Society of Friends. He died about 1691. His group first began to gather about 1650. The Quakers are dedicated to the morals and ethics of Scripture and are also guided by the Inner Light of Christ residing in every person. One common vein in Quaker belief is conscientious objection to military service. Since their inception, the Quakers have been recognized as a peace church. They migrated to America seeking religious

---

[101] Merrill, Peter, C., *German Immigrant Culture in America*

freedom in the late 1600's and early 1700's. In America they continued their pacifist convictions.

A sample of the codified convictions of Quakers regarding this topic is the following section quoted from the *Declaration of Faith* issued by the Richmond Conference of 1887, under the heading of Peace:

> We feel bound explicitly to avow our unshaken persuasion that all war is utterly incompatible with the plain precepts of our divine Lord and Law-giver, and the whole spirit of His Gospel, and that no plea of necessity or policy, however urgent or peculiar, can avail to release either individuals or nations from the paramount allegiance which they owe to Him who hath said, "Love your enemies." (Matt 5:44, Luke 6:27) In enjoining this love, and the forgiveness of injuries, He who has brought us to Himself has not prescribed for man precepts which are incapable of being carried into practice, or of which the practice is to be postponed until all shall be persuaded to act upon them. We cannot doubt that they are incumbent now, and that we have in the prophetic Scriptures the distinct intimation of their direct application not only to individuals, but to nations also. (Isa 2:4, Micah 4:1) When nations conform their laws to this divine teaching, wars must necessarily cease.
>
> We would, in humility, but in faithfulness to our Lord, express our firm persuasion that all the exigencies of civil government and social order may be met under the banner of the Prince of Peace, in strict conformity with His commands.

With the Revolutionary War, the attitude of other American settlers changed toward the peaceful Quakers. For failure to join the regiments against the British, Quaker COs (conscientious objectors) were imprisoned and their property confiscated; some were heavily fined.

The Quakers found themselves in the same dilemma with the outbreak of the Civil War in America. Many young members of the sect not well founded in their persuasion joined the armed forces. The patriotic zeal and anti-slavery sentiment was more compelling for them than the archaic religion of their forefathers. The CO (conscientious objector) Quakers were in a minority. Abraham Lincoln's administration provided for COs, and a person claiming to be a conscientious objector had to pay $300 to circumvent military service, a sizeable amount at that time. Still others were forced into service by ruthless military commanders, or had property confiscated as a type of persecution for refusing inscription.

During both World Wars and all wars since, the Quakers have been firm in their conviction as conscientious objectors. They also have offices available for conscientious objection counseling. During World War 1, 13 Quakers were courts-martialed and sentenced to incarceration for refusing induction into the armed forces. During World War 2, 951 Quakers were COs and assigned to civilian public service. During the Vietnam War, Friends provided 600 COs in 1968, 1,700 COs in 1969, and 2,300 COs in 1970.

50   THE CHURCH OF THE BRETHREN

The church of the Brethren, also known as the Dunkers, began in 1708 in Germany with an original group of 8 persons. In 1719, the group under the leadership of Peter Becker came to America and accepted free land offered by William Penn, and the settled in Germantown, PA. Additional families arrived from Germany as time timed and the group spread across the country. Their membership at present is about 170,000.

The original tenets of the Brethren include their opposition to war and military service. In their *Statement of the Church of the Brethren on War* from their 1970 Annual Conference, they state,

The official position of the Church of the Brethren is that all war is sin and that we seek the right of conscientious objection to all war.

The Church of the Brethren since its beginning has repeatedly declared its position against war, and their understanding of the life and teaching of Christ as revealed in the New Testament led their Annual Conference to state in 1785 that they should not "submit to the higher powers so as to make ourselves their instruments to shed human blood... The church cannot concede to the state the authority to conscript citizens for military training or military service against their conscience."

Morally the Brethren opposed the Revolution and they were against slavery as well during the Civil War era. Their pacifist convictions have continued since their arrival in America and throughout all wars since then. The church provides counseling for all military age members to be conscientious objectors, but also pledges its support for constructive civilian work as alternative service. The church also teaches that their members should not have employment or investment in defense industries. During World War 1, 24 Brethren were courts-martialed and sentenced to incarceration for refusing induction into the armed forces. During World War 2, 1,352 Brethren were COs and assigned to civilian public service.

A branch of the Brethren known as the Old German Baptist Brethren (Old Order Dunkers) are also conscientious objectors. According to their tenets, "Any member who enters military service will fall into the judgment of the Church." Non-cooperation in political and secret societies is also required of the members of the Dunkards.

51   THE DUKHABORS

The concepts held by the Dukhabors of Russia are documented beginning about 1734 during the reign of Empress Anna. The Dukhabors repudiated the rites and theology of the Russian Orthodox Church, were pacifist and refused military service in the army of the Tsar of Russia. Their leader Ilarion Pobirokhin and his followers migrated to the Tambov region about 1760, and from which center the Dukhabor philosophy spread throughout Russia. The Dukhabors as a religious entity were exiled from central Russian by Tsar Pavel I, in 1802, to the southern Ukraine and Caucasus regions of Russia.

The tenets of the Dukhabors were codified in 1791 in a confession of faith that was presented to Governor Kakhovski of Ekaterinoslav. Tenet XVII pertains to war:

> Dukhabors want to extend this spirit of peacefulness to both those of their community and to enemies; and war is prohibited, affirming the evangelic teaching of love toward enemies. Matt 5:38-39.[102]

An important event in Dukhabor history is the burning of arms on June 29, 1895, advised by their leader at the time, Peter Vasilivich Veregin. Much like the decree of universal military service of his father, Tsar Alexander III required an oath of allegiance from all his subjects in Russia. As a protest to this requirement, which the Dukhabors would not fulfill, they gathered all their weapons, those used for hunting, or personal collections, and destroyed them in large bonfires. Dukhabors again began to refuse orders to take up weapons or participate in military exercises. Needless to say, they were severely persecuted. Eventually the Dukhabors migrated from Russia to

---

[102] Livanov, Feodor Vasilich, *Raskolniki I Ostrozhniki*, vol. 2, chapter IV, (translated from the Russian by the author.)

Canada seeking religious freedom and the ability to live as conscientious objectors.

52 LEO N. TOLSTOY

The famous Russian author Lev Nicholaevich Tolstoy made the concept of Christ's teaching on non-violence and non-resistance to aggression the theme of his book, *The Kingdom of God is Within You*. It was first published in 1893, and immediately became popular among the many sectarian groups in Russia. The book was a result of Tolstoy's personal conversion and study of Christ's teachings. In later years, Tolstoy incorporated his philosophy in his novels.

Tolstoy served in the Russia army, 1855-1856, in the Crimean War against Turkey, and personally experienced the horror of organized warfare and the bloodshed of the battlefield. This experience impressed upon him the futility of the objectives of armed struggle and the senselessness of the many wounded and dead in battle. His study of the gospels and especially the Sermon on the Mount in later years converted him to pacifism. The concept of Tolstoy in this book was that the divine kingdom as taught by Jesus Christ was antithetical and alien to military service. The 2 concepts were of 2 different domains: one of the divine kingdom and the other of the secular government.

> Christianity in its true significance annuls the state. So it was understood from the very beginning, and for this reason Christ was crucified, and people who were not bound by the obligation of justifying the Christian state understood it in this manner. Only from the time of the acceptance of a nominal and superficial Christianity by the heads of states did there begin the contrivance of all of these improbable cunningly-woven theories, which allowed the compatibility of Christianity and the state. But for every sincere and serious person of our era there

cannot but exist an apparent incompatibility between true Christianity – the teachings of humility, forgiveness of offenses, love – and the state and its supremacy, violence, executions and wars. The profession of true Christianity does not only exclude the possibility of the acknowledgement of the state, but annuls its foundations.

I know regarding myself that I do not need to attack other nations, killing them, neither do I need to defend myself from them with a weapon in my hands, and so I cannot participate in war or the preparation for it.[103]

His book did influence many, explaining that the only acceptable conduct of a true follower of Christ was that of non-violence and especially not resorting to retaliation or aggression. The person in whom the kingdom of God resided was not to succumb to the politics of national struggle and ideology of military service. To Tolstoy, peaceful coexistence with all other individuals, societies and nationalities was attaining an earthly kingdom of God. Tolstoy's attitude of non-violence and pacifism was influential on many religious and political leaders of the 20th century.

53   SEMEON UKLEIN AND THE MOLOKANS

The primary preceptor of the Russian Molokans was Semeon Matveeich Uklein, who preached from 1760 to 1805 throughout central Russia. Uklein was son-in-law of the Dukhabor leader Ilarion Pobirokhin, and lived with him in the same village. Uklein was evangelical in contrast to the philosophic Pobirokhin, and later separated from his father-in-law and joined the Molokans, who like the Dukhabors, were conscientious objectors.

---

[103] Tolstoy, Leo, *The Kingdom of God is within You*, chapter 10.

Uklein, along with Matvei Semeonich Dalmatov, compiled a confession of faith of the Molokan religion. Point 23 of his teaching is the following:

> About oaths and war. Fulfilling the divine commandments, they [Molokans] do not have need for human ones, and must escape the fulfillment of those laws which are contrary to the teaching of the Word of God. So they must, for example, escape servility to landowners, war, military obligation, and oaths, and matters not permitted by the Holy Scriptures.[104]

Historically the Russian Molokans have been conscientious objectors, and over the years have suffered imprisonment and exile for refusing to join the military. As a result of their pacifist convictions, Molokans would not participate in the mandatory conscription imposed by Tsar Alexander III in the years 1887-1889. Rather than opposing any further persecution by the Tsarist government, they migrated out of Russia to America in the years 1904-1911.

In America the Molokans have continued in their convictions as conscientious objectors, refusing military service in both World Wars and subsequent wars. During World War 1, 6 Molokans were courts-martialed and sentenced to incarceration at Ft. Leavenworth Federal Penitentiary for refusing induction into the armed forces. During World War 2, 76 Molokans were COs and assigned to civilian public service, while about 20 were absolutists and were incarcerated at various prisons, including Terminal Island Penitentiary, CA, McNeil Island Penitentiary, WA, Ft Leavenworth, and Tucson State Penitentiary, Tucson, AZ. About 80 Molokans were CO during the Vietnam War.

---

[104] Livanov, vol. 2, chapter XII.

54   STUNDISTS

The sectarian movement of Stundism was the result of the influence of German Mennonite colonies on residents of Ukraine. The appellation of Stundist is derived from the German word "stunde," meaning hour, because German Anabaptists gathered to study the Bible at specific hours of the day, which the local Russians and Ukrainians also began to do.

Karl Bonekemper, a German Anabaptist preacher in the village Rohrback, in Kherson Province, Ukraine, distributed New Testaments in the vernacular Russian to local Ukrainians and invited them to read them. The residents noticed a difference between the ROC and Anabaptists teachings. As more New Testaments were distributed, more residents read them, and the German pastors spread their Protestant views even more. Stundists were already meeting independently by 1862, and had incorporated the Mennonite tenet of objection to military service into their own.

A report was issued by Attorney-General of the Holy Synod Konstantine Pobedonostsev identifying the Stundists as a denomination very detrimental to Russian society, and he recommended that they be forbidden to conduct services. The circular letter distributed to Orthodox churches was dated September 3, 1894, and it stated the following:

> The adherents of the sect of the Stundists, rejecting all ecclesiastical rites and sacraments, not only do not recognize any authorities and oppose oaths and military service, but are similar to those criminals undermining the defenders of the fatherland, and who preach socialist principles, for example material equality, distribution of possessions, and etc., and their teachings tear at the root of the basic principles of the Orthodox faith and Russian nationalism.[105]

Soon after the beginning of World War I, the ultra-patriotic paramilitary groups began to attack denominations that were conscientious objectors to military service, and especially the Stundists in Ukraine, labeling them German agents and traitors. Stundists eventually assimilated into the general Baptist denomination in Russia.

55   EARLY RUSSIAN PENTECOSTALISM

Pentecostalism migrated to Russia via the Evangelistic and Pentecostal revival work of Wesleyan Methodist minister Thomas Barrak in Norway in 1906, which expanded quickly into Finland. Pentecostalism in Russia, in the form that it is known at present, was introduced by A.I. Ivanov.

Ivanov resided in Helsinki in 1908–1910, attended Pentecostal revivals there, and himself preached to Russian-speaking residents living in Helsinki as well as at a church in Vyborg, north of St. Petersburg. Ivanov moved to Petersburg in about 1910, with his family, and began preaching Pentecostalism in St. Petersburg. Much like the Russian sectarians of earlier generations, Ivanov taught objection to military service as part of his gospel. Everything was going well until some sailors of the Russian Imperial Navy accepted his gospel. These born-again Pentecostals refused service on their ship on June 19, 1915, and they were immediately taken into custody and court-martialed. The former sailors were sentenced to various terms at hard labor camps, distant from central Russia.

Refusal of military service by members of the Imperial Navy due to new religious convictions was alarming to imperial authorities. They considered Ivanov's preaching to be anti-military and opposed to the interests of the Russian government, and in November 1915, Ivanov and several Pentecostal ministers

---

[105] Shubin, Daniel H., *History of Russian Christianity*, Vol. 3, pgg. 160-163.

of Petersburg were arrested. They were sentenced to a long-term exile to a remote area in the geographical center of present-day Kazakhstan, and their history ends at this time. The reaction at the Methodist Church headquarters in Helsinki was likewise negative: Ivanov and the other ministers were excommunicated in absentia from the Evangelical Christian Church, and they were labeled cowards.[106]

56   THE CHRISTADELPHIANS

This denomination originated here in America under Dr. John Thomas. He came to America from England about 1833 and joined the Disciples of Christ, studying the Bible under the Cambellites. He discovered the inadequacies of historic Christianity and broke away starting his own congregations in about 1848. He taught a return to primitive Christianity, and conscientious objection to military service was one of their tenets. The Christadelphians were conscientious objectors during the Civil War and have been since that time. Thomas' convictions were continued under the preacher Robert Roberts.

> The Christadelphians do not believe in participating in war. So, when the Civil War broke out, they refused to go. In order to be recognized as a religious group that did not believe in fighting, they needed a name. Dr. Thomas gave them the name "Christadelphian" which, in Greek means "Brethren of Christ."[107]

During World War 1, one Christadelphian was courts-martialed and sentenced to incarceration for refusing induction into the armed forces. During World War 2, 127 Christadelphians were COs and assigned to civilian public service.

---

[106] Shubin, ppg. 179-180.
[107] Christadelphian History (www.carm.org)

57   JEHOVAH'S WITNESSES

Properly titled the Watchtower Bible and Tract Society, they are labeled as a cult by historical Christianity because of their refusal to accept several tenets of ecumenical Christendom as Biblically-valid. One of the main criticisms is that the JWs are non-secular. They do not pledge allegiance to the flag or serve in the armed forces, and have been heavily persecuted as a result of this in America and in other countries. The JWs are the largest single absolutist group in America.

> Following the examples set by Jesus and first-century Christians, Jehovah's Witnesses do not share in the politics or wars of any nation. Their stand of Christian neutrality is well documented in history. They firmly believe that they must "beat their swords into plowshares" and not "learn war anymore." (Isaiah 2:4)[108]

During World War 1, 27 JWs were courts-martialed and incarcerated for refusal of induction into the armed forces. During World War 2, of the 6,086 conscientious objectors who were absolutists, or who refused civilian public service as an alternative to military service and were subsequently tried and convicted and sentenced to incarceration, 4,441 were JWs. Of the 12,000 COs who accepted civilian public service during WW2, 409 were JWs.[109]

Two examples of war hysteria creating suspicion and eventually prosecution of JW conscientious objectors will be provided. The first occurred during WW1 and involved the leader of the International Bible Students Association (Jehovah's Witnesses), Joseph F. Rutherford, and 7 members of his

---

[108] Office of Public Information of Jehovah's Witnesses
[109] Keim, Albert N., *The CPS Story*, pgg. 8, 81.

denomination. The matter that initiated the prosecution was the following passage in Pastor Charles Taze Russell's book *The Finished Mystery*:

> Nowhere in the New Testament is patriotism (a narrowly minded hatred of other peoples) encouraged. Everywhere and always murder in its every form is forbidden. And yet under the guise of patriotism civil governments of the earth demand of peace-loving men the sacrifice of themselves and their loved ones and the butchery of their followers, and hail it as a duty demanded by the laws of heaven.

The passage was determined by the courts to be a violation of the Espionage Act of June 15, 1917, since it promoted, as the judge determined, non-registration and refusal of induction into the armed forces. Judge Joseph F. Rutherford, who led the JWs subsequent to Pastor Russell, and 7 other members of the denomination, were sentenced on June 21, 1918 to 20 year prison sentences at a federal penitentiary. However, after one year of incarceration at the Federal Penitentiary at Atlanta, GA, a Court of Appeals reversed the conviction and the men were freed. Clergy of mainline denominations rejoiced at the conviction of the JWs, and especially because of their view that JWs were a non-orthodox religious body, and the same clergy became disappointed when the conviction was reversed.[110]

The second example provided occurred during WW2 and is documented in 3 US Supreme Court Decisions: one unsuccessful, two successful. War hysteria still existed during WW2 toward religious groups that were opposed to war and military service, but in a more subtle manner.

Every serious Witness considers himself a full-time minister of the Gospel, even though such work of proselytization is actually accomplished in their spare time, all of them also

---

[110] Abrams, Ray H, *Preachers Present Arms*, pgg. 184-186

holding regular jobs. Because of this claim, the JWs who received conscription notices during WW2 expected to receive an exemption as ministers (class IV-D, Minister of Religion). The local draft boards either refused their requests entirely, which subjected the JW to arrest for refusing induction, or else would assign them CPS, which many also refused based on the premise that such an assignment interfered with and removed them from their ministry.

As a result several JWs filed lawsuit in local federal courts, and all of them inevitably lost on a regular basis. Three of the court cases, however, managed to reach the US Supreme Court. The first important one was Falbo v. United States, 320 US 549 (1944). Nick Falbo refused to report to a CPS camp to fulfill alternative service, after being refused an exemption as a full-time minister, and was sentenced by Federal Court to 5 years in prison. The Supreme Court upheld the conviction because Falbo did not exhaust the normal channels of repeal, but went directly to filing a lawsuit in Federal Court. Justice Black delivered the majority opinion of the court on January 3, 1944: they expected Falbo to enter CPS camp, and while there proceed to further appeals.

A second court case was Estep v. United States, 327 US 114 (1946), and the political environment had somewhat changed now that WW2 was over. William Estep and Louis Smith (their cases were decided together) refused to report for induction, claiming the local draft board had erred in refusing them ministerial exemptions. Estep and Smith were tried in a Federal Court in 1944 and found guilty of Selective Service law violations. The 3rd Court of Appeals upheld the decision. Justice William Douglas wrote the majority decision (decided February 4, 1946) and stated the following regarding the impropriety of conduct of both the local draft board and District Federal Court:

> He was indicted for willfully failing and refusing to submit to induction. He sought to defend on the ground that as a Jehovah's Witness he was a minister of

religion and that he had been improperly denied exemption from service, because the classifying agencies acted arbitrarily and capriciously in refusing to classify him as IV-D. He also claimed that the right to an effective appeal had been denied because the local board unlawfully withheld certain relevant documents from the appeal board and included improper material in the record on appeal. The District Court rejected these defenses and did not permit the introduction of evidence to sustain Estep's conviction. The jury found him guilty and he was sentence to imprisonment for term of 5 years.

The Supreme Court overturned the decision of the lower court, but ordered that a new trial be held with better consideration of the evidence that the JWs would provide. Of course, the case was then dropped.

A second modest victory for the JWs was in Gibson v. United States, 329 US 338 (1946). The case of George Dodez was argued at the same time. Both were denied IV-D exemptions as full-time ministers and were assigned to CPS camps. Taze Gibson deserted CPS camp after he arrived there for assignment, was arrested and tried for Selective Service law violation, and found guilty. George Dodez, like Falbo above, never arrived at CPS camp, and was likewise tried and found guilty in Federal Court. The matter proceeded to the US Supreme Court and Justice Rutledge delivered the majority opinion of the court:

> Nothing in this section or the statue, in the light of our prior decisions, can be taken to indicate that Congress intended persons charged with violating such duties (i.e. refusing CPS) to be deprived of their rights of defense on the ground of invalid classification...

The decision of the Supreme Court overturned the verdict of the earlier courts for both men, and then required a new trial with their opportunity to provide testimony that would prove them full-time ministers. Their cases were both dropped since WW2 was long over.

In retrospect the length of sentences delivered to JWs for Selective Service law violations – refusing induction or refusing CPS – averaged 40 months, about 7 months longer than others of mainline Christian denominations who were tried and found guilty of the same violations.

58   BERTRAND RUSSELL

A section on Bertrand Russell is included in this treatise because of his life-long dedication to the area of anti-war protest and effort and intervention to curb warfare during the 20th century, while at the same time, able to discredit the entirety of Christendom due to their lack of intervention into this matter. Russell stated emphatically that he did not believe in God, and that he was not Christian.[111] Yet Russell, wrote book after book upholding pacifist principles, intervening between world leaders to reconcile them and to convince them of the futility of deliberate war, and protested regularly against arms proliferation and the use of nuclear weapons.

Russell in his early years was a mathematician, with a very pragmatic and rational mind, but a mystical experience molded his morality and ethic for the balance of his life. He describes this in his *Autobiography*.

> Suddenly the ground seemed to give way beneath me, and I found myself in quite another region. Within five minutes I went through some such reflections as the following: the loneliness of the human soul is unendurable; nothing can penetrate it except the highest intensity of the sort of love that religious

---

[111] Russell, Bertrand, *Why I am not a Christian*, pg. 5

teachers have preached; whatever does not spring from this motive is harmful, or at best useless; it follows that war is wrong, that a public school education is abominable, that the use of force is to be deprecated, and that in human relations one should penetrate to the core of loneliness in each person and speak to that.[112]

Much like Tolstoy who, after reading the Gospels, was driven to create a Christian philosophy based on the basic principles of the Sermon on the Mount, Russell was affected in the same manner, but to develop a pacifist philosophy based on humanitarian and political principles. The repulsion of Russell toward Christianity appears to be due to his annoyance over Christians' failure to observe the most basic tenets that were taught by Jesus Christ.

You will remember that He said: "Resist not evil, but whosoever shall smite thee on thy right cheek, turn to him the other also." That is not a new precept or a new principle. It was used by Lao-Tse and Buddha some 500 or 600 years before Christ, but it is not a principle, which as a matter of fact, Christians accept.[113]

...religion prevents us from removing the fundamental causes of war;[114]

Bertrand Russell succeeded in doing for Jesus Christ what his disciples of the 20th century would not – and could not – do, which was to actively protest war and be willing to suffer the consequences for it. Russell – the non-Christian – was a greater benefit to the cause of Christian pacifism than any Christian leader of his era.

---

[112] Russell, Bertrand, *Autobiography, 1872-1914*, pg. 234.
[113] Russell, Bertrand, *Why I am not a Christian*
[114] Russell, Bertrand, *Has Religion Made Useful Contributions to Civilization?*

59   PACIFISM IN LATER HISTORY

One author that should be quoted here because of his silent but positive impact on conscientious objection during the Vietnam War era is Thomas Merton. He was a theology student in 1943 when he was called up for conscription during WW2, and so he applied as a non-combatant, but he was rejected during the medical examination for not having enough teeth. Merton then became a Trappist monk and withdrew from the world to a life of contemplation. Merton developed a repulsion toward war while watching events unfold in Europe beginning 1939, and wrote the following:

> I knew that I myself hated war, and all the motives that led me to war and were behind war. But I could see that now my likes or dislikes, beliefs or disbeliefs meant absolutely nothing in the external, political order. I was just an individual, and the individual had ceased to count. I meant nothing in this world, except that I would probably soon become a number on the list of those to be drafted. I would get a piece of metal with my number on it, to hang around my neck, so as to help out the circulation of red-tape that would necessarily follow the disposal of my remains, and that would be the last eddy of mental activity that would close over my lost identity.[115]

Two other important leaders of the Reformation period who were Christian pacifist will also be mentioned. Casper Schwenkfeld (1487-1541) was originally a Lutheran, but later rejected their doctrine, and began teaching doctrines similar to those of the Quakers. Sebastian Franck (1499-1542) was a Catholic monk and rebelled against the sacraments and organization of the Catholic church. In addition to objection to war he also taught

---

[115] Merton, Thomas, *The Seven Story Mountain*, pg. 214.

religious tolerance and abhorred persecution of those labeled heretics.[116]

Herbert Armstrong's Worldwide Church of God was originally pacifist, a result of Armstrong's early Quaker upbringing and his own personal study of the Bible. Those who attended his Ambassador College were exempt from conscription because they were considered divinity students.

There are many small denominations in America that adhere to pacifist convictions, and many more in history past, but which could not all be mentioned here. The above examples are provided as evidence that throughout Christian history, from the apostolic age and to the present, there have always been those who believed in the concept of the divine kingdom accompanied by the conviction of conscientious objection to military service. Although small in number they retain a place in history for refusing to conform to the demands of the state and pressure from militarist Christian denominations regarding military service.

Even then, members of historical peace churches have occasionally strayed from the tenets of their faith and joined the military, but these are the exception; likewise adherents of major pro-military Christian denominations have also voiced disapproval of warfare at various occasions and have refused to serve, much to the dismay of their religious leaders. There are also many non-religious bodies that utilize political or philosophical arguments as their refusal to serve in the military or earn a living in some military industry.

---

[116] Christie-Murray, David, *A History of Heresy*, pg. 166.

CHAPTER SIX

AMERICAN MILITARIST CHRISTENDOM

"It is God who has summoned us to this war. It is his war we are fighting... This conflict is indeed a crusade. The greatest in history—the holiest. It is in the profoundest and truest sense a Holy War...Yes, it is Christ, the King of Righteousness, who calls us to grapple in deadly strife with this unholy and blasphemous power."
Rev. and retired Civil War Confederate Army Field Chaplain Randolph H. McKim, from the pulpit at the national capital, World War One.[117]

60   MILITARIST CHRISTENDOM AND THE MEXICO WAR AND THE CIVIL WAR

Little information is available regarding the relationship of churches to the Mexico or Spanish-American War of 1846-1848. The following is a selection from a popular history of the United States:

> The churches for the most part were either outspoken for the war or timidly silent. Generally, no one but the

---

[117] McKim, Randolph H., *For God and Country*, pg. 116-117

Congregational, Quaker and Unitarian churches spoke clearly against the war.[118]

During the Civil War, major Christian denominations offered their patriotic support to the either the Union or the Confederacy, depending on the location of their congregation. As a result, members of the same denomination were killing each other on the battlefield, both supported by their respective ecclesiastical leaders.

> The Methodists, Baptists, Congregationalists, Lutherans, Catholics, Moravians, German and Dutch Reformed, Old and New School Presbyterians tired to outdo each other in declaring their undying allegiance to the Federal Government. The Methodists took great pride in their record of one hundred per cent loyalty.[119]

> In the Confederacy, most of the churches supported the South. The Presbyterians, in session in 1862, were convinced that "this struggle is not alone for civil rights, and property and home, but for religion, for the church, for the Gospel."[120]

For the most part, the division of the denominations was based on their view toward slavery: the southern churches defending the practice, having a good basis for it in the Bible, while the northern churches were favoring abolition. With the Emancipation Proclamation and the defeat of the Confederacy, the southern churches' doctrines were modified to fit the new legislation. Likewise, as the Union army invaded the Confederacy, ministers of several mainline denominations were on their tail, taking possession of churches.

---

[118] Zinn, Howard, A People's History of the United States, pg. 156
[119] Abrams, Ray, *Preachers Present Arms*, pg 5.
[120] Abrams, pg. 6.

61   MILITARIST CHRISTENDOM AND WORLD WAR 1

Germany declared war on Russia on August 1, and against France on August 3, 1914, and in response, Great Britain declared war on Germany on August 4. As a result of the war in Europe, arms manufacturing began in the USA due to the fear of possible invasion and for America to be prepared in case it was drawn into the war. The attitude of Christian denominations oscillated from complete support of war preparation and without reservation, to a refusal of preparation or entrance into a European war under any circumstances.

Then a German submarine sunk the Lusitania on May 7, 1915, and attitudes quickly changed. The denominations with ties in Great Britain and France, such as the Presbyterians, Baptists, Methodists, Congregationalists, and Episcopal, quickly modified their gospel. The Lutherans were in a dilemma and the attitude varied from member to member. Cardinal Gibbons spoke on behalf of the Catholic Church, and felt the entrance into war not necessary just because a few Americans were killed in the sinking of the Lusitania. Gibbons felt that the Americans should have known better than to travel on the open seas in European waters during wartime.[121] But then on the day before American's declaration of war against Germany, Gibbons changed his viewpoint entirely and urged Catholic young men to join the military.

On April 6, 1917, the USA declared war on Germany, and one by one the ecclesiastical leaders and denominations that were earlier fervent advocates of peace and supportive members of peace organizations succumbed to supporting the war effort and sending the military age members of their respective congregations to Europe. When in January 1915, the Church Peace Union had a response of 95% against war preparation, but by March 1916, the united effort of many ecclesiastical leaders suppressed the efforts of the Union, and for the balance of the

---

[121] Abrams. pg. 30.

war it was no longer effective. By April 1917, all of the 30 or so peace societies had succumbed to war frenzy and capitulated to supporting the war effort, except for a small remnant of the Church Peace Union. On the day following the declaration of war, officials of the Federal Council of the Churches of Christ were already laying plans for the best method of cooperating with the US government and supporting the war effort.

> Frederick Lynch, one of the founders of the Church Peace Union, and editor of the *Christian Work*, was one of the most ardent peace men in America, if not in the world... He worked against our entrance into the war up to the very last. But once in the fray he was calling the Germans Huns and baby-killers with gusto.... Dr. Lynch said that out of his wide acquaintance with peace men he could think of hardly a dozen out of hundreds who were not loyally supporting the war.[122]

Ministers who were skeptical about the war support of their denomination were caught in the frenzy or else were pressured by their peers and their congregation to support the recruitment activities. It was either conforming to the patriotic trend of the era, or risk losing their positions and face ostracism.

> What else could they have preached other than that the boys in the trenches had found God? To have remained silent or to have pointed out the spiritually devastating effect of warfare would have cost them their leadership and their jobs. The churches demanded ministers who gave comfort and dogmatic assurance, and they received it...[123]

---

[122] Abrams, pg. 55.
[123] Abrams. pg. 61.

The most difficult situation was the metamorphosis of the Prince of Peace, Jesus of Nazareth, into a soldier. The same rhetoric of the medieval theologians who justified the Crusades and inquisitions echoed from the pulpits of America. They called Jesus the lion of the tribe of Judah whom every American should emulate by laying down his life for his brethren on the battlefield. The preachers modified the passages referring to spiritual warfare to that of physical warfare, and encouraging them to give to Caesar what belonged to God as their greatest sacrifice. The purpose of Jesus during wartime was not to send peace, but a sword, and it was time to take the sword out of its sheath. Over and over the Germans were equated with the incarnation of evil, and their defeat was the victory over sin. Books of sermons for wartime were written and sold and preached from in order to excite military-age members of their congregations into either joining the service or supporting the war effort. The most repulsive and imbalanced of sermons was that of Edward Dosworth, Congregational minister and dean of Oberlin College, who preached that taking a life in war was the Christian thing to do:

> The Christian soldier in friendship wounds the enemy. In friendship he kills the enemy. In friendship he receives the wound of the enemy. He keeps his friendly heart while the enemy is killing him. His heart never consigns the enemy to hell. He never hates. After he has wounded the enemy he hurries to his side.[124]

Lyman Abbot, a Congregationalist clergyman and editor of the Christian magazine, *The Outlook*, claimed in 1914 that he was a member of every peace society in the USA, but as with other clergy, his attitude changed with the entrance of America into World War 1. At this time, Abbot recommended that, "every Christian church should be a recruiting office for the Kingdom of

---

[124] Abrams. pg. 67.

God. The Christian Church and the Christian ministry should hear the voice of the Master saying, I have come not to send peace, but a sword. And they should lead Christ's followers forth, his cross on their hearts, his sword in their hands."[125]

Of all the clergy of America during WW1, it was William Ashbury "Billy" Sunday, a Presbyterian evangelist famous for his hell, fire and brimstone tirades, who promoted the war effort against the Germans more than any other single Christian clergyman,. Billy Sunday would pray in his revivals asking God to "guide the next gunner who sights a U-boat so that his aim will be true." At the same time he promoted the sale of war bonds. The following are a couple of samples of his performed sermons:

> "Our little trouble with Spain[126] was a coon hunt as compared with this scrap we have on hand with that bunch of pretzel-chewing, sauerkraut spawn of blood-thirsty Huns ... We can win, we must win. We shall win, so dig down deep and let us fill Uncle Sam's bank vault high with our money and help send a shiver down the crooked spine of the Hohenzollerns who are dancing on this thin crust of hell, and thus let the guns of the army and navy to dig their graves; then the world can live in peace."[127]

> "The man who breaks all the rules, but at last dies fighting in the trenches, is better than you Godforsaken mutts who won't enlist."[128]

During WW1, pastors and priests who were supposed to be more objective in their rational as a result of their theological training and respect as men of God were swept away by war hysteria and mob influence just as did the most base and servile residents of

---
[125] Abrams, pg. 83.
[126] i.e. Spanish-America War of 1898.
[127] Abrams, pg. 112.
[128] Abrams, pg. 106.

the US. Such clergy only exposed themselves as being unfit for leadership in time of moral crisis, and embarrassed themselves in the sight of their parishioners, unable to adhere to the precepts they claimed were so valuable to them in times of peace.[129]

As the recruitment increased American Christendom increased its support of the war effort. Many churches opened their doors and became recruitment offices for the US military, while ecclesiastical elders were sent into local neighborhoods to makes lists of men of military-age to provide to the recruitment officers. American Christendom had abandoned its purpose as the preacher of the gospel of Jesus Christ the Prince of Peace, and became the means for preserving American state policy and the military concept of might is right. Every denomination in America followed the dictates of the state except for the few historic peace churches and a few small denominations. The victory in the end, however, was not as they had expected.

The mainline denominations only gained a shallow and empty victory with the end of WW1, as soldiers returned from the front, and as many did not return but were buried somewhere in Europe in shallow graves. Disillusioned clergy admitted their myopic vision of divine involvement in the war, as Frederick Lynch again oscillated in his attitude toward war.

> Our people, government and all, were shouting wonderful things that were going to come to pass as the result of this war. It was a war to end war. It was to make the world safe for democracy. It was to make a new world order where Christian principles were to reign among nations. There is no denying that we are in a disappointed world – a world that looks back upon the men who were at Paris as betrayers of their words and promises.[130] We got no world safe for democracy, no new world order, no Christian era of international good-will.[131]

---

[129] Abrams, pg. 247.
[130] i.e. the Versailles Treaty, June 28, 1919.
[131] Abrams, pg. 234

Many other clergy followed suit in public repentances of their earlier advocacy of military intervention and their involvement in war hysteria.

> Charles Clayton Mossison, who as editor of *The Christian Century* had pronounced his blessing upon the war, has now for several years been calling upon the churches to renounce war forever, and advises that "the preachers repentantly resolve that they will never again put Christ in khaki or serve as recruiting officers or advisory enforcers of conscription laws."[132]

Eliot Porter, a Presbyterian clergyman who acted as a chaplain on the front lines for the British armed forces, refused any further advocacy of war and the ministry of the chaplain corps. Stephen Wise, a rabbi from New York who earlier supported military-age male Jews in the American armed forces, likewise repented of such conduct, and pledged without reservation never to bless or support war or any war whatsoever again. Thousands of clergy made public their new conviction, learned as a lesson from WW1, that in the future they would not sanction any war or the participation in it of any armed combatant.[133]

Harry Emerson Fosdick, originally a Baptist preacher and professor at the Union Theological Seminary, New York, and later pastor of the First Presbyterian Church in the City of New York, 1918 to 1925, heartily endorsed the war and provided considerable theological justification for it, as he stated, "Even Jesus did not bless the peaceful; he blessed the peacemakers; and peace-making in any human relationship may any day involve resort to force." But then after the conclusion of the war, he retracted his position, stating, "I do not propose to bless war again, or support it, or expect from it any valuable thing."[134]

---

[132] Abrams, pg. 237
[133] Abrams, pg. 238
[134] Abrams, pgg. 133, 235.

However, it is not as though Germany did not have its own prominent theologians and religious leaders who provided divine approval for their own soldiers in fighting against American soldiers. Paul Tillich, who became a very influential Protestant theologian and author of many books on the history of Christian theology, was a military chaplain during WW1 in the German army. Tillich would tell his soldiers in the field, "We are fighting for our fatherland and we are fighting for God." Tillich, the military chaplain, believed in German victory and felt that by Germans fighting on the battlefield they would gain eternal salvation. But as the war progressed, Tillich watched his fantasy of victory devolve into defeat, and as a result his attitude changed from a vehement militarist to a pacifist. In the 1920s, Tillich supported religious socialism and pacifism. He eventually lost his professorship at the University of Frankfurt when Adolph Hitler ascended to power in 1933, and then migrated to America. With WW2, Tillich again changed his attitude, and supported the US armed forces in the war against Germany.[135]

Pastors in the year immediately following Armistice realized that their support of the war effort materialized because they were caught in the flood of patriotism unleashed by the US government, fearing reprisal should they refuse to approve the edicts of congress and the declaration of war, and fearing the loss of their position as pastor should they speak out against militarism in their congregations while facing the parents and offspring of those who had joined the military to fight the war to end all wars and to make the world safe for democracy. Pastors wanted the favor and approval of their peers, government officials, and their parishioners by being willing to stand up for America, that love of country transcended love of humanity, that democracy was a divine institution as opposed to other forms of government, and especially, that God was on the side of the

---

[135] Bergen, Doris, *The Sword of the Lord: Military Chaplains from the First to the Twenty-First Century.* Article by Hartmut Lehmann, pg. 138.

Americans, and not on the side of the enemy Huns, and America had to prove it on the battlefield.

62 MILITARIST CHRISTENDOM AND WORLD WAR 2

The reaction of American mainline denominations to World War 2 was similar in pattern to that of World War 1: pacifism or neutrality was their initial official stance, advocating distance from the problems of Europe. However, after the day of infamy, December 7, 1941, the attitudes quickly changed and now were inclined towards intervention. Because many preachers who were caught in the hysteria of WW1 were either alive or still in their pulpits, remembering the events of the era, how they echoed the voice of Congress, the attitude now was considerably more cautious. The rhetoric was considerably more scholarly in support of the "good war," with educators such as Reinhold Niebuhr providing divine approval to the war.

If the motto of WW1 was to make the world safe for democracy, for WW2 it was the good war to protect democracy from its defeat by fascism. American Christendom had merged the protection of democracy with the protection of the institution of Christianity, and which also meant the defeat of the institution of Christianity should democracy be defeated. Gerald Sittser described it as follows:

> These leaders thus identified themselves as the religious guardians of the nation's heritage. They laid claim to America as their own. Because they believed that America's future depended upon the Christian faith, they felt obligated as the leaders of the church to take responsibility for America... The church's identity, in other words, became attached to the nation's destiny.[136]

---

[136] Sittser, Gerald, L., *A Cautious Patriotism*, pg. 255-256.

The concept of Christian pacifism was acceptable to the population of America during the peacetime interval between the two world wars, during the depression. But now with the aggressor's attack on American soil, Pearl Harbor, preachers recovered from their pacifist tendencies to present themselves loyal to American intentions. Much as with WW1, mainline denominations were too interwoven into the fabric of American economy, polity, and society to deny enlistment to the military-age men and women of their congregations. Freedom of religion was a witness to the divine favor of God toward America, and parishioners felt that the motto of "In God we trust," caused America to have a special place in God's heart. The vast majority of denominational officials supported the war effort: they provided chaplains for the military, produced recruits from among their congregations, comforted those who lost a member of a family in the war, and sermonized about the evils of fascism and benefits of democracy. Christians worked at military industries manufacturing weapons and invested their savings into war bonds. In reality, it was democracy that was the real religion of American – life, liberty, and the pursuit of happiness – and the institution of denominational Christianity was its divine materialization. If democracy was defeated, so would be Christianity, the pulpits declared, because democracy depended upon Christianity for its survival and success.

The official stance of the Methodist Church in 1940 toward the possibility of war with Germany was stated in their *Doctrines and Discipline*:

> Therefore we stand upon this ground: The Methodist Church, although making no attempt to bind the consciences of its individual members, will not officially endorse, support, or participate in war. We insist that the agencies of the Church shall not be used in preparation for war, but in the promulgation of peace.[137]

However, Methodist officials in 1944 completely reversed their attitude:

> In this country we are sending over a million young men from Methodist homes to participate in the conflict. God himself has a stake in the struggle, and he will uphold them as they fight forces destructive of the moral life of man. In Christ's name we ask for the blessing of God upon the men in the armed forces, and we pray for victory. We repudiate the theory that a state, even though imperfect in itself, must not fight against intolerable wrongs.[138]

The Lutheran Church of America followed close behind:

> Therefore, we call upon our people in particular, and all Christian people in general, to dedicate themselves wholly, with every resource of heart and mind and conscience, to the defeat and destruction of this evil.[139]

The response of Catholics, Baptists, Presbyterians, and other mainline denominations followed the same vein, as they issued proclamations at their conferences on the necessity of vanquishing the evil empire of fascist Germany, and which was echoed in the pulpits of their congregations.

Once the Allies gained military ascendancy over the central axis and Japan, America initiated incendiary bombing of major cities: Berlin, Dresden, Hamburg, Tokyo and Hiroshima. Prior to his time, the bombing had been precision, strategic bombing

---

[137] *Doctrines and Discipline of the Methodist Church*, 1940, Statement on Peace and War, par. 1716 (III), pg. 777.
[138] *Doctrines and Discipline of the Methodist Church*, 1944, The Christian Church and War, par. 2016, pgg. 574-575.
[139] *Minutes of the Thirteenth Biennial Convention of the United Lutheran Church*, 1942, pg. 145.

concentrated on military bases, communication centers, and industrial areas, in order to cripple the enemies' war operations. Now however, the military changed its policy to incendiary bombing, loss of the millions of innocent civilians – men, women, children, and elderly – that were now annihilated in the ruthless devastation. The incendiary bombing of Tokyo killed over 1 million people in 2 days, far more than the nuclear bombs exploded over Nagasaki and Hiroshima. The goal was to hasten the end of the war, regardless of the means. Gerald Sittser described the response of Americans and America's churches upon hearing of the new military tactics:

> Though German cities received the first blows of America's obliteration bombing, Japanese cities felt its full force. The (US) air corps simply abandoned precision bombing and began to conduct massive incendiary raids against city centers in Japan. The public applauded, largely because of the racial bias against the Japanese that had been smoldering in America for decades and finally flared up during the war.
>
> Like the general population, most American Christians supported the massive bombing of German and Japanese cities, and the churches for the most part remained silent on the issue.[140]

Charles Clayton Morrison, writing in the *Christian Century*, defended the military strategy of incendiary bombing of civilian centers, because, as he felt, once America's Christian churches supported America in the war effort, it had no choice but to concede to the military the type of weapons and tactics they felt were necessary in order to gain the soonest victory. He refuted one American liberal, who opposed such bombing, in the following manner:

---

[140] Sittser, pgg. 217-218

It appalls us to say this, but it must be said: bombing, if it contributes to victory, is here to stay as long as war lasts. Those who merely raise the moral and humanitarian questions are talking in a vacuum.[141]

The voice of a few clergy that did raise protest was ignored by the state. The fact that Christians in the military, and the US Chaplain Corps included, violated one of the primary criteria of Augustine's justifiable-war theory – which was that only military personal should be the target and not civilian – was irrelevant. Of the 45 million that were killed during World War 2, 30 million were civilians, and 15 million were military personal. The loss of the millions of civilian population residing in enemy territory was not an issue as far as gaining the victory at the earliest was concerned.

63 MILITARIST CHRISTENDOM AND THE VIETNAM WAR

The primary denominational support of the Vietnam War was the evangelicals, whose policy was voiced through their mouthpiece, the National Association of Evangelicals (NAE). It was their conviction that war was the proper manner of halting communist aggression, and they insisted on nothing short of complete victory. Billy Graham – who will be further discussed – was a vocal supporter of military might to gain a victory in Vietnam, and stated his views in his *Decision* magazine. Other evangelical leaders who were avid supporters of military intervention into Vietnam were John R. Rice, Army veteran of WW1, fiery evangelical preacher and editor of *Sword of the Lord* magazine, who labeled conscientious objectors and antiwar protesters as friends of communism; Catholic Archbishop of New York Francis Cardinal Spellman, who referred to US troops in Vietnam as "soldiers for Christ"; Carl H.F. Henry, editor of

---

[141] Sittser, pg. 218.

Christianity Today magazine; Harold John Ockenga, the primary founder and president of the National Association of Evangelicals; Christian author and Baptist preacher Harold Lindsell, who stated, "All Americans, and especially Christians, should stand by the President [Nixon], even if they think his policy is mistaken;" and Billy James Hargis, founder and director of Christian Crusade Ministries, who was a vehement anti-communist. In 1969, the Reverend Jerry Falwell referred to the soldier fighting in Vietnam as a champion for Christ.[142] Following in the footsteps of Billy Graham, Falwell advocated a militarily-strong American, which he felt would defend the country from the threat of atheist communism. He equated American military supremacy in the world with God's favor on the country: invincible both spiritually and militarily.

Articles in *Christianity Today* submitted by prominent evangelicals supported the intensive bombing of North Vietnam, and referred to any civilian deaths or destruction of private property as "regrettable." John Rice wrote in his book *War in Vietnam* regarding the soldiers recruited to fight:

> Nothing can be clearer than that God sometimes approves of people going to war for principles and that He is with them, and when they call on Him and trust Him, He will give them victory and deliverance.

The fiery radio preacher Carl McIntire organized a series of Victory in Vietnam marches in Washington, DC, from 1969 to 1972, and claimed that COs were the "voice of Hanoi," who hindered the war effort and promoted disobedience among American citizens. McIntire stated in one of his sermons:[143]

> It is the message of the infallible Bible that gives men the right to participate in such conflicts, and to do it

---

[142] Bacevich, *The New American Militarism*, pg. 127.
[143] Loveland, *American Evangelicals and the U.S. Military*, pg. 119-122.

with all the realization that God is for them, that God will help them, and that if they believe in the Son of God, the Lord Jesus Christ, and die in the field of battle, they will be received into the highest heaven.

As active their voice was in support of state policy regarding Vietnam, so active was their voice against conscientious objection to military service. As Anne Loveland described it:

In the midst of the debate over Vietnam, such thinking led evangelicals to denounce antiwar protesters, especially those identified with mainline religion, almost as harshly as the fundamentalists did. If they did not go so far as to label them communists or communist sympathizers, they did not hesitate to charge them with giving "comfort to Communist aggressors." And the words and phrases they used to describe mainline antiwar protesters – "The neo-Protestant ecumenical establishment" and "secular theologians of social revolution" – implied a logical connection between their ideological and theological heresies.[144]

It was only out of respect to historic pacifism that evangelicals and mainline denominations condoned conscientious objection, but the bulk of their literature evaded the early Christian stance. As an example, the Methodist Church continued its oscillation between militarism in WW1, pacifism in the interval, and then militarism again during WW2; and then condemning war in 1944, after the horror of the war in both Europe and the Pacific theaters was brought home. In the 1968 edition of *The Book of Discipline* of the Methodist Church, the new stance with the progress of the Vietnam War very active was ambivalence:

---

[144] Loveland, pg. 124.

Therefore, the Church recognizes the right of the individual member to answer the call of his government according to the dictates of his conscience and his sense of duty. It also recognizes the right of those who for the sake of conscience feel they cannot participate in war in any sense whatsoever.[145]

The Methodist denomination could not make a firm stand in favor of Christian pacifism, and still had to include a statement that actually placed service to the state above that of the individual decision to be a CO.

64   MILITARIST CHRISTENDOM AND THE IRAQ WAR

Wars have an origin, and which are usually political and economic in nature, and so with the present Iraqi War. To understand the Bush-Halliburton connection with the invasion and war, we need to go back 15 years to the Kuwaiti war. After the defeat of Iraq, it was placed under economic sanctions by the US, and the northern 1/3 and southern 1/3 became "no-fly" zones. The elder President George H.W. Bush hoped that economic deprivation - embargo - of Iraqi residents would break the back of the government, rather than further war. But this did not occur. Instead, countries in Europe, like France, that need petroleum (since their countries do not produce it), made arrangements with Iraq to buy their oil in Euros once the embargo was lifted. During the 12 years of embargo, Iraq reverted into a poverty-stricken 3rd world country and without the ability to manufacture any weapons of mass destruction. The 8-year war with Iran also depleted their economy.

    Of course, once the US government heard about the arrangements between European nations and Iraq, plans were started to use war to take over Iraq, so the US could acquire the

---

[145] *Book of Discipline*, 1968, pg. 66

oil and US dollars would be used, instead of Iraq selling oil to Europe and getting Euros for it. Preparations for a war against Iraq began about half-way through the second term of the presidency of William Clinton, about 1998.

Since Cheney once was the CEO of Halliburton, a company involved in the petroleum industry, he was the primary candidate for Vice-President, now with the proposed war against Iraq already in the planning. Since Saddam Hussein was a dictator, the US plan was to walk in, depose the dictator, be hailed as heroes, and take over the petroleum industry under the administration of Halliburton, so the US could handle Iraqi oil in US$, instead of Iraq selling it to Europe in Euros. Of course, the propaganda to justify invasion that the Bush-Cheney team fed the American population was the weapons of mass destruction that Saddam Hussein was supposed to be harboring and manufacturing, which was a lie.

The catalyst to starting the invasion was the tragic Twin Towers attack of Sept 11, 2001, even though no Iraqi association could be proven. Nonetheless, the US congress and the naive American public went along with the plan.

But the lesson of Vietnam meant nothing to these US military brass and government officials, that foreign countries do not want the help of America with their internal problems, regardless of their severity. This would equally extend to middle-eastern Islamic countries: they do not want Americans to interfere with their personal national politics either. America at present is doomed to remain in Iraq, even with the consequences of over 4,000 American soldiers dead, 24,000 wounded, many American civilians executed by Iraqi anti-American forces, over 100,000 Iraqi civilians dead (some accounts raise the figure to as high as 650,000), and the devastation of their country, economy and civilization. American military and political leaders know that they cannot leave Iraq, because if the US does leave, after the end of the civil war that will definitely occur, they know that the Iraqis will sell their oil in Euros to European countries. By keeping the US army there, and at whatever cost in lives, and deceiving the Americans telling them that the Iraqis want democracy, Bush-Cheney have a chance at Iraqi oil in US$. This is not a good situation for the US, and will not end anytime soon, and nobody knows what the result will be. War is money, politics and power, and it is a massive deception for the US government to tell us that US soldiers are there fighting to protect our freedoms. The soldiers are there to protect and give their lives for American big business, just as with Vietnam.

At the present, the same evangelical leaders that advocated Vietnam as a military defense against the spread of atheist communism repeat the same lines from 30 years ago, except that Islam has replaced atheistic communism. With the old enemy having fallen by the wayside with the dissolution of the Soviet Union in 1990, collapsing from the self-induced weight of its own inefficient bureaucracy and godless society, a new enemy has emerged, against which the evangelicals have rallied together. In October 2002, almost 70% of conservative Christians favored military action against Iraq, as opposed to 54% of the general US population. One example is the following editorial published October 23, 2003, a few months following the invasion of Iraq:

> Not to be outdone in cashing in on the violent clash of good versus evil and the fears of their flocks are televangelists like Pat Robertson, Jerry Falwell, and Franklin Graham, who view the escalating carnage in the Middle East, Iraq, and Afghanistan as Biblical prophecy pitting the forces of their righteous Judeo-Christian God against the evil God of Islam.[146]

Not to be left behind in the dust, Charles Colson, likewise a member of the conservative Christian right, and founder of Prison Ministries, voiced his view, based on his political-

---

[146] Turnipseed, Tom, *Good Versus Evil Sells Violence to Serve the American Empire*, www.commondreams.org,

ecclesiastical perspective of the justification of a pre-emptive strike on Iraq:

> Christians should remember that the just-war doctrine is not grounded in revenge, punishment, or even justice. Thomas Aquinas discussed it in Summa Theologica – not in the section on justice but in the section on charity, that is, the love of God. Out of love of neighbor, then Christians can and should support a preemptive strike, if ordered by the appropriate magistrate to prevent an imminent attack.[147]

This is an example of the imbalanced rationale that was supplied to President G.W. Bush and military and political officials by prominent Christian leaders to justify attacking Iraq, even when no evidence existed of a possible and premeditative attack on the part of the Iraqis.

In the perspective of the adherents of mainline Christian denominations and evangelical Christians, America will prove militarily that the Christian God is greater than the Islamic Allah, even if it needs to entirely destroy the nation of Iraq, including its population, culture and ancient civilization. This perspective was fine for Old Testament Israel, as the proceeded to defeat the 7 nations of Canaan on their entrance into the promised land, or the defeat of the Philistines under the early kings, but it does not apply to the era of the gospel of the Prince of Peace, to overcome evil with good.

---

[147] Christianity Today, December 9, 2002, *Sometimes going to War is the Charitable thing to do*.

65   THE CHURCH OF JESUS CHRIST OF THE LATTER-DAY SAINTS

Among the major denominations of America, the Mormons are historically the most patriotic. The 12th Article of Faith, written by Joseph Smith in 1842, reads:

> We believe in being subject to kings, presidents, rulers, and magistrates, in obeying, honoring, and sustaining the law.

Obligatory military service is stated as official ecclesiastical doctrine.

> The Church considers being loyal citizens to be a duty of its members, irrespective of nationality. Responding to a call for military service is one appropriate manner of fulfilling this duty of citizenship.[148]

The earliest military service of Mormons was 500 who volunteered to serve in 1846 in the war against Mexico. During the Civil War, their involvement was negligible due to the isolation of the Utah communities, although a few served in the Spanish-American War, and more in WW1. In 1940, Mormon president J. Reuben Clark, Jr. encouraged the enlistment of military-age Mormons when conscription was legislated in 1940, stating, "We shall confidently expect that no young male member of the Church will seek to evade his full responsibility."[149]

Conscientious objection is not recognized by the Latter-Day Saints, and is discouraged. The basis for Mormon patriotism and military service follows the vein of Biblical exegesis similar to that of historic Christendom.

---

[148] MacMillan's Encyclopedia of Mormonisn, Vol. 4.
[149] Oaks, Robert C., *Military and the Church*

66 THE CHURCH OF THE NEW JERUSALEM

The tenets that Emmanuel Swedenborg provided for the denomination that he founded included their attitude toward war and military service. The following are the 2 passages from Swedenborg's final and culminating treatise regarding his religion, *True Christian Religion*, written in 1771.

407. Wars that have as an end the defense of the country and the church are not contrary to charity. The end in view declares whether it is charity or not.
414. Natural needs relate to civil life and order, and spiritual needs to spiritual life and order. That one's country should be loved, not as one love himself, but more than himself, is a law inscribed on the human heart; form which has come the well-known principle, which every true and endorses, that if the country is threatened with ruin from an enemy or any other source, it is noble to die for it, and glorious for a soldier to shed his blood for it.[150]

The above passages leave the final decision up to the conscience of the individual. As much as Swedenborg was a mystic and seemed to have transcended the physical realm and the material world, yet his conclusions on such a vital issue as war are shallow and inconclusive. During Vietnam era, the Swedenborg Church did support the young men of their congregations that decided to apply as COs.

67 C. S. LEWIS

A section on Clive Staples Lewis is included in this treatise to provide to the reader an example of the type of arguments that

---

[150] Swedenborg, Immanuel, *True Christian Religion*, vol. 1, pg. 614, 619.

contemporary Christians utilize to justify war. Some of his arguments are based on the over-repeated advice of John the Baptizer to soldiers, the centurion of Matt 8, and Cornelius. The balance of arguments uses the rational of the necessity of armed combat to vanquish a greater enemy for the benefit of the state, regardless of the means necessary to accomplish this. Lewis' thoughts on Christian militarism are published in his essay *Why I am not a Pacifist*, which is the text of an address he gave in Oxford, England in 1940 for pacifists of Great Britain – Bertrand Russell no doubt included, even if indirectly – to change their convictions and support the war effort.

In general Lewis just shrugs aside and ignores all the commands of the NT regarding peace, reconciliation, toleration of offenses, and the spiritual warfare as opposed to the physical. As much as a Christian apologist Lewis considers himself, for him to turn to reason and philosophy in his arguments is self-defeating, because the conclusion of any matter based purely on reason is no more valid for one person than for another.

> The main contention urged as fact by pacifists would be that wars always do more harm than good. How is one to find out whether this is true?... That wars do no good is then so far from being a fact that it hardly ranks as a historical opinion.[151]

Lewis takes lightly the event of taking a person's life in war, and does not take seriously that soldiers deprive people of their sole conscious existence. Lewis is wrong in his statements, because the matter must be viewed objectively: all that a person has is his life, and because of this, strict laws are legislated and enforced that prohibit the arbitrary deprivation of a person of his life. So therefore, the argument for not taking a person's life is on the side of the person himself, and laws are so written that the burden is on the killer or executioner to justify killing a

---

[151] Lewis, C.S. *The Weight of Glory*, pg. 73

person or executing capital punishment. In the same vein, the burden is on the militarists to prove that by expending money and labor to build armaments; by creating an army; by having the army place itself in danger of losing the lives of its own soldiers – or perhaps even defeat; by systematically killing the enemy – innocents included; and devastating his country; that in the process a greater good or benefit will be accomplished than if warfare was adamantly refused. It is the military – not the pacifists – that must justify the death of every person that is killed, as well as the death of every soldier of its own, to prove that this was a greater benefit that if they never proceeded to war.

It is an unassailable and unavoidable historical fact that wars have caused innumerable deaths, endless suffering, and the devastation of property and civilizations. Such logic of Lewis that it is only a historical *opinion* that wars do no good is absurd and ludicrous. Then he reverses his logic in the following statements:

> It seems to me that history is full of useful wars as well as of useless wars.[152]
> Nor am I greatly moved by the fact that many of the individuals we strike down in war are innocent. That seems, in a way, to make war not worse but better. All men die, and most men miserably.[153]

How can war be made better with the death of innocent men, women and children? A normal person would expect such rhetoric from a fascist or communist, not from a Christian apologist, since Christ came not to destroy people's lives, but to save them.

---

[152] Lewis. pg. 74
[153] Lewis. pg. 75

> And war is a very great evil. But that is not the question. The question is whether war is the greatest evil in the world, so that any state of affairs which might result from submission is certainly preferable. And I do not see any really cogent arguments for that view.[154]

Whether war is the greatest evil is not the question, but whether war is evil at all. And if it is evil, then this is justification to abstain from it, as the Apostle Paul wrote, "Abstain from every form of evil." 1 Thess 5:22. Reconciliation is always better than succumbing to evil, as Jesus said, Blessed are the peacemakers, in the Sermon on the Mount.

Lewis then turns to authority to supplement his defense of militarism. But he does not turn to Biblical injunctions of the NT, but to secular figures who are of no consequence in the sight of God.

> If I am a pacifist, I have Arthur and Aelfred, Elizabeth and Cromwell, Walpole and Burke, against me. I have the literature of my country against me, and cannot even open my *Beowulf,* my Shakespeare, my Johnson, or my Wordsworth without being reproved.[155]

> To be a pacifist, I must part company with Homer and Virgil, with Plato and Aristotle, with Zarathustra and the Bhagavad-Gita, with Cicero and Montaigne, with Iceland and Egypt.[156]

To begin with, such figures have no place in a debate of the Scriptural basis of this matter, or in any theological discussion at all. If Lewis was Christian to begin with, he should have long ago departed company with pagan philosophers. Every one of

---

[154] Lewis. pg. 78
[155] Lewis. pg. 80
[156] Lewis, pg. 81

these authors and philosophers depart from Christian truth and have no place to begin with in a Christian defense of militarism.

Lewis then turns to what he claims to be religious authority. He admits that if he was to base his convictions on exclusively the teachings of Jesus Christ, he has no defense. But to serve as a denominational defense, he turns to the teachings of his own Church of England.

> Looking at the statement which is my immediate authority as an Anglican, the Thirty-Nine Articles, I find it laid down in black and white that "it is lawful for Christian men, at the commandment of the Magistrate, to wear weapons and serve in the wars."[157]

Since Lewis is Anglican, the Thirty-Nine Articles are divine authority as far as he is concerned. But the head of the Church of England is the King or Queen of England, and during the era of the 16th and 17th centuries, if the church did not support the policy of the sovereign by justifying service in the armed forces, the bishops would have been quickly expelled and replaced by others who would acknowledge the supremacy of the sovereign in ecclesiastical and doctrinal matters.

The final statements of Lewis are:

> It may be after all that pacifism is right. But is seems to me very long odds, longer odds than I would care to take with the voice of almost all humanity against me.[158]

The Apostle Paul said, "Let God be true though all people be liars." Rom 3:4. Even if all humanity speaks in defiance of a person's conviction, contrary to a person's tenets, and in any matter, not just in the matter of Christian pacifism, all that matters is if God is the truth in the matter. "But if God is with

---

[157] Lewis, pg. 83
[158] Lewis. pg. 90

you, who is against you?" Rom 8:31. All humanity justifying an action that is a violation of the precepts of the Gospel is a futile argument and of no consequence. All that matters is NT gospel truth. This attitude would likewise apply to any other topic or action where the state or population opposes the individuals with firm convictions in the ethic and morality of the NT.

Such shallow and weightless arguments of Lewis, echoed over and over in so many circles of Christian theologians and educators, have only caused war to continue without end in sight, since they offer no reason to stop any war in progress on in planning.

68   REINHOLD NIEBUHR

Reinhold Niebuhr was a prominent theologian in liberal circles during the decade before, during, and after World War 2. He provided more than any other clergyman divine justification of the American war effort against Germany. Niebuhr's early years were spend as a pastor at an evangelical church in Detroit, and later he became a professor at Union Theological Seminary in New York. Much like the many other mainline denomination preachers of World War 1, Niebuhr was swept away in the support of the war effort, but then after WW1, when he faced the effects of his decisions, he also repented of his participation, saying, "The times of man's ignorance God may wink at, but now he calls us to repent. I am done with this business."[159]

Niebuhr visited French-occupied Germany in 1923, which confirmed his newly-formed stance of Christian pacifism, now seeing first-hand what the Allied invasion did to Europe, as well as the impact that the Treaty of Versailles had on the economy and population of Germany. Up until the rise of Adolf Hitler in Germany in 1932, Neibuhr was a confirmed pacifist, but then his

---

[159] Abrams, pg. 235.

stance again changed. The very attitude that Niebuhr disavowed in 1923 he again embraced, and he wrote in 1932:

> The best means of harmonizing the claim to universality with the unique and relative life of the nation, as revealed in movements of crisis, is to claim general and universally valid objectives for the nation. It is alleged to be fighting for civilization and for culture; and the whole enterprise of humanity is supposedly involved in its struggle.[160]

The new Niebuhr was converted into a political philosopher, who now considered Christianity as the defender of western civilization, and he evolved into a vehement opponent of pacifism. The ethics of Jesus could not be applied to the real world, claimed Niebuhr, because of the domination of sin, and all of the ethical teachings of the NT were now subject to the circumstances of the progress of history and became relative issues. The new purpose of the Christian church was to protect democracy from defeat by fascism, and so protect western civilization from devolution into tyranny, as Sittser describes him:

> Niebuhr assumed that the United States could live in this tension of confidence and humility, justice and repentance only if the church in America was strong, visionary, and active. The immediate purpose of the war – victory over Germany – was a horrible business, though necessary for the sake of western civilization.[161]

In February 1941, Niebuhr founded a new magazine titled, *Christianity and Crisis*, to bring to the attention of readers the crisis that American was facing. The crisis, as Niebuhr defined

---

[160] Niebuhr, Reinhold, *Moral Man and Immoral Society*, pg. 97.
[161] Sittser, Gerald L., *A Cautious Patriotism*, pg. 75

it, was the ideology and aggression of Nazi Germany, which was a threat to American democracy and freedom. The crisis was growing as a result of America's reluctance to declare war against Germany and so defend Christian civilization.[162]

Niebuhr ignored in its entirety the NT basis for pacifism, claiming that it was impractical and inapplicable to politics in the real world of global conflicts. Pacifism, as far as Niebuhr was concerned, was heresy, and it made Christianity unfeasible in the real world. Niebuhr simultaneously ignored the reasons that pacifists gave for their view, even though he had been one earlier. He refused to acknowledge the fact that pacifists were sincere in their goal to be faithful disciples of Jesus, who also had lived in the same sinful world that we live in. Niebuhr likewise ignored the reason why many of his contemporary theologians continued to adhere to pacifism: they informed him that it was the results of the prevalence of sin in society that forced them to take this stance, feeling that it would reduce violence, reprisal and hatred.

The post-war goal of Niebuhr in America was social justice, and which he proposed for the defeated countries after World War 2. Even though Niebuhr considered himself an evangelical theologian, he was much closer to being a social activist based on humanist philosophy.

69   WILLIAM FRANKLIN GRAHAM

Billy Graham was to the Vietnam War, what Billy Sunday was to WW1, and what Reinhold Niebuhr was to WW2: divine approval of military methods to defeat an enemy and condoning military aggression. If there is any epitaph that Billy Graham wants in order to be remembered for his life on earth, it is his posts of spiritual advisor to nine Presidents of the United States and unofficial pastor of the White House. Over a period of 50

---

[162] Sittser. pg. 2.

years, from Harry Truman to William Clinton, Graham was a regular visitor to the White House, especially during the terms of Richard Nixon and Lyndon Johnson. Graham was unable to succeed with Truman, but did with Eisenhower, the hero of WW2, even giving a benediction at his inauguration. Graham likewise attended the first of many presidential prayer breakfasts, the first occurring February 1953, attended by some 500 senior members of the US government.[163] Many, however, viewed the close superficial friendship between the evangelist and the presidents as each one promoting the agenda of the other for personal gain. Many conservative preachers criticized him, claiming that he told the presidents what they wanted to hear, and Graham wanting in return their approval of him and their promotion of his evangelistic crusades. The evangelist enjoyed the prestige he acquired as being unofficial pastor and spiritual advisor to the presidents. Graham supported Eisenhower in his campaign for the presidency, and also Nixon in his presidential race against John Kennedy. But Graham did not draw near to Kennedy, because he was Catholic.

The elementary flaw in the theology of Graham is that he "always acknowledged that he saw no lasting solution to most of the world's problems short of the second coming."[164] Such a nihilistic and pessimistic view of Christian involvement in the world – that it will always be ineffective due to the insurmountable task ahead – led Graham to preach a shallow and dilute gospel that had little strength in motivating believers to do any more than the absolute minimum. Such a conviction weakened his message as it pertained to social advancements, as well as precluding war. Responsibility could also be evaded for failure to address critical sins, because such sins will always be and there is nothing you can do about it. And since there will be wars and rumors of wars, as Jesus said, then there is nothing that can be done to curb it, short of the second coming of Christ.

---

[163] Loveland, Anne C., *American Evangelicals and the US Military, 1942-1993*, pgg. 40-41.
[164] Martin, William, *A Prophet with Honor: The Billy Graham Story*, pg. 362.

During the many visits of Graham to the White House during the Vietnam War years, never did he tell either President Nixon or Johnson to stop the war, or stop the aggression, or stop the bombing, but rather voiced his support of American foreign policy. Graham preached that because communism was atheist, it was a threat to the existence of freedom of religion in America, just as fascist Germany in WW2 was a threat to democracy. When questioned about his support of Johnson's foreign policy, Graham's response was, "My only desire is to minister to our troops by my prayers and spiritual help wherever I can." Upon his return to the US after visiting Vietnam, Graham praised the heroic efforts of American troops, endorsing the war against communism, even though privately he knew that America was not winning. Such a dilute gospel of biased indecision only continued the war and devastation in Vietnam. At no time during his visit to Vietnam did Graham tell the troops to cease warfare, nor could he, even when other clergyman urged him to beseech President Nixon to stop the bombing of North Vietnam.

> In justifying US intervention in Southeast Asia, Graham and other evangelicals appealed to the domino theory and the principle of containment. In 1965, after combat troops had been dispatched to Vietnam, the evangelist declared at a press conference, "We are dealing with naked aggression... Communism has to be stopped somewhere, whether in is in Hanoi or on the West Coast. The president believes it should be stopped in Vietnam."[165]

William Martin noted the manner that Graham reduced the seriousness of war in 1973, toward the end of the Vietnam War. Graham was quoted as saying:

> "We say that the slaughter in Vietnam has been terrible, but we lose more people in one month on the highways of

---

[165] Martin, pg. 124

America than the total Vietnam war has cost us. So it's safer to be fighting in Vietnam than driving on the highways."[166]

"A thousand people are killed every week on the American highways, and half of those are attributed to alcohol. Where are the demonstrations against alcohol?"[167]

Regardless of the validity – even though his statistics are not completely accurate – this is still no justification for the Vietnam war. Both alcohol and war are wrong, but a lack of protest against alcohol does not justify war. The following statement appeared as part of an article in the New York Times of April 9, 1971:

"I have never heard of a war where innocent people were not killed. Tens of thousands of innocent people were killed at Hiroshima and Nagasaki."[168]

But Graham was not ignorant about the evil of war, and especially the carnage and annihilation occurring in Vietnam as a result of his 2 trips to the country. Graham visited Vietnam twice, in Christmas of both 1966 and 1968. Instead of going there for a crusade as a means of curbing the spread of communism, as he did to Moscow in 1984, and in other Iron Curtain cities of eastern Europe, Graham went to motivate the troops to continue their military struggle, as he stated on his return.

"The stakes are much higher in Vietnam than anybody realizes. Every American can be proud of the men in uniform who are representing our nation on that far-flung battle front. They are paying a great price for the victory they are almost certainly winning there."[169]

---

[166] Martin, pg. 347
[167] Martin, pg. 423
[168] Loveland, pg. 162.

But he never told them to put down their weapon or to overcome evil with good. War, as Graham considered the matter, was a political issue, which he felt that he should not address. But yet from the other side of his mouth, he encouraged Americans to support the soldiers, and said, "There is no question: the war is won militarily."[170]

As a result of Graham's indecision on Vietnam, many denominational clergymen were disenchanted with his political gospel. One southern Baptist preacher, Will Campbell, labeled Graham "a false court prophet who tells Nixon and the Pentagon what they want to hear." While I.F. Stone called him, "a smoother Rasputin."[171] A few of Graham's Southern Baptist friends felt the evangelist, as the Charlotte, NC, *Observer*, quoted, "is too close to the powerful and too fond of the things of this world," and they compared Graham "to the prophets of old who told the kings of Israel what they wanted to here."[172]

Nonetheless, Graham ignored the criticism and rather aligned himself further with President Nixon. In May 1970, at his crusade held at the University of Tennessee stadium, just 10 days after the killings of innocent students at Kent State University, Kent, OH, Nixon appeared on the podium with Graham. Nixon also addressed the crowd of thousands that evening. Graham told the crowds that evening as he stood next to Nixon on the podium, "I'm for change – but the Bible teaches us to obey authority." Such a statement was an excuse for Graham to elude his responsibility to uphold Biblical morality and ethic by claiming submission to state authority. Graham's statement also indicated that state authority had the supremacy over Biblical authority, even if the state was advocating a matter that was opposed to the morality and ethic of the Bible, warfare and military aggression in this case. A small contingent of anti-

---

[169] Martin, pg. 345.
[170] Martin, pg. 347.
[171] Martin, pg. 361.
[172] Martin, pg. 387.

war protesters who attempted to voice their dissatisfaction of what appeared to be Graham's capitulation to Nixon's war policy, and preferred him to use the occasion to censure the war, were restrained by Secret Service agents and drowned out by the applause of the crowds. Pathetically, both Graham and Nixon each achieved their respective goals that evening.[173]

When the threat arose that some 4,000 of his Crusaders might be conscripted into the military, which included a large number from Bill Bright's Campus Crusade for Christ, all of a sudden the patriotism of Graham faded into the background. Although they were not ordained ministers, yet Graham contacted Nixon at the White House, requesting that they all receive exemptions as full-time ordained ministers, to exempt them from conscription. The response from the White House was for Graham not to worry about this matter.[174] (Yet the same attitude was not extended toward Jehovah's Witnesses, who were likewise in the same situation.)

Prior to launching the invasion of Kuwait on January 17, 1991, Graham was invited to the White House by President George H.W. Bush for a meeting, and then Graham returned the next day, and he and the president went to the Pentagon, adjacent to Fort Myer, where the evangelist led a prayer service on behalf of superior military officials. On January 28, 1991, just 2 weeks later, when President Bush spoke at the Annual Convention of the National Religious Broadcasters in the presence of such popular American evangelists as Billy Graham, Jerry Falwell, Pat Robertson and James Dobson, he publicly lauded Graham for his support of the administration's policy:

> But above all, we will prevail because of the support of the American people, armed with a trust in God and in the principles that make men free – people like each of you in this room. I salute Voice of Hope's live radio

---

[173] Martin, pg. 368-369.
[174] Martin, pg. 360.

programming for US and allied troops in the Gulf, and your Operation Desert Prayer, and worship services for our troops held by, among others, the man who over a week ago led a wonderful prayer service at Fort Myer over here across the river in Virginia, the Reverend Billy Graham.

Graham's association with the presidents did not terminate when they left office. To further consolidate his reputation as White House pastor, Graham gave the eulogy at the funeral for President Richard Nixon on April 27, 1994, lauding him with the words:

> On behalf of the family of Richard Nixon, I welcome you who have gathered to join with them in paying final respects to the memory of Richard Milhous Nixon, the 37th president of the United States. Today, in this service, we remember with gratitude his life, his accomplishments, and we give thanks to God for those things he did to make our world a better place.

If any event testifies to Graham's surrender to the foreign policies of the US government in order to receive the approval and favor of the administration in return, it is his receipt of the Sylvanus Thayer Award in 1972. The US Armed Forces reciprocated the effort made by evangelical leaders for their promotion of US policy in Vietnam with public displays of recognition. The award is given annually to an accomplished citizen of the US, whose effort coincided with the principles expressed by the motto of the US Military Academy West Point: Duty, Honor, Country.[175] Graham accepted the award on May 4, 1972 and was lauded by West Point officials. The presentation of the award to Graham at West Point also directly implied their appreciation for his support of the military and government

---

[175] Bacevich, pg. 140

foreign policy in regards to Vietnam. In response as part of his address to the students and faculty of West Point, Graham advocated military intervention to suppress the spread of communism.[176] Graham told the cadets exactly what they wanted to hear: criticism of anti-war protest and demonstrations, and equating the ideals that West Point stood for with Christian ideals that were necessary for the success and strength of the nation.[177]

70   THE AMERICAN CHRISTIAN RIGHT

The decrease in militarism in America in the years following Vietnam dismayed evangelical Christian leaders, that the reduction in military strength would remove or reduce God's favor. The conclusion was based heavily on Old Testament ideals: blessings of God upon Israel occurred when the nation was strong, under Joshua, David, Hezekiah, and this equally applied to America. In no manner, evangelicals felt, should America be second in military strength, especially second to atheist and communist Soviet Union. As a result, Jerry Falwell, along with Jimmy Swaggert, Jim Bakker, and an assortment of other evangelical leaders created the Religious Coalition for a Moral Defense Policy. The primary purpose of the new group was to persuade the US Congress to pass the Strategic Defense Initiative, also known as Star Wars project. These evangelical ministers, and the millions of US population and thousands of supportive Christian clergy – felt that such military strength – making America the supreme world power – would draw God's favor upon America, as it now had the means to protect itself – its form of democracy and religious freedom – from the threat of atheistic communism.[178] (Although the Soviet Union was already fragmenting at this time and collapsed just a few years later.)

---

[176] Loveland, pgg. 165-166.
[177] Bacevich, pg. 141.
[178] Bacevich, pg. 137-138.

In the modern era, the same figures repeat the same lines of 20 years ago, except that Islam has replaced atheistic communism. Richard Cizik, vice-president for the National Association of Evangelicals, told the *New York Times* on May 27, 2003, "Evangelicals have substituted Islam for the Soviet Union."[179] With the old enemy having fallen by the wayside, collapsing from the weight of its own inefficient bureaucracy and godless society, a new one has emerged against which the evangelicals have rallied together. A few months prior to the invasion of Iraq, on January 11, 2003, Jerry Falwell announced at the Grace Baptist Church, Knoxville, TN, "Fighting in Iraq is a just war." Falwell also added that, "we should pray for American military personnel and the type of warfare – whether biological, chemical and nuclear – they'll face in the Middle East." Such rhetoric further facilitated war rather than reconciliation.

Another area that merged evangelical religion into the state is the intrusion of several para-church groups into military society. Beginning during the late 1960s, prayer groups, Bible studies, and breakfasts and luncheons with religious overtones, became regular at the Pentagon and military bases. Christian study groups were then formed within these military establishments. Some of these groups that promoted the institution of Bible study and fellowship groups within the military enclaves were the Full Gospel Business Men's Association,[180] Campus Crusade Military Ministry (associated with Campus Crusade for Christ), the Billy Graham Evangelistic Association, Officers Christian Fellowship, and the Navigators. These on-base military Bible study and fellowship groups all had military officers as their directors or presidents. The detriment of this intervention of evangelical religion into the military was that war and military service was accepted as the norm, while the idea of Christian pacifism and the tenets of the divine

---

[179] Kaplan, Esther, *With God on their Side*, pg.13
[180] The grandfather of Demos Shakarian was an Armenian Pentecost and also a Christian pacifist.

kingdom were considered un-American. The vocation of the soldier was never refuted, but was equated with the warrior of Christ, but against the earthly enemies of the state. The religion promulgated in the enclaves of military bases by evangelicals was not the religion of Jesus, but that of Plato.

One example of the merge of church and state in a religious revival was Explo 72, held in June 1972, in Houston, TX, sponsored by Campus Crusade for Christ; Billy Graham was honorary chairman. The welcome address was given by Major General Gerhard Hyatt, chief of US Army Chaplains. The military officials who attended and participated in the crusade took advantage of the crowds to diffuse the severity of death and devastation in Vietnam, while Campus Crusade for Christ included support for the US military as part of its agenda. However, when antiwar Christians, such as the People's Christian Coalition and the Mennonite delegates, attempted to distribute antiwar literature, they were harassed. The participation of military officials at Explo 72 illustrates their support of evangelical religion.[181]

This mutual relationship between evangelical religion and the military continued into the future decades with their mutual cooperation in support of increasing America's military arsenal and eventually the first war in Kuwait and the present Iraq War. The perplexing paradox can be summarized in the words of Andrew Bacevich:

> Conservative Christians have conferred a presumptive moral palatability on any occasion on which the United States resorts to force. They have fostered among the legions of believing Americans a predisposition to see US Military power as inherently good, perhaps even a necessary adjunct to the accomplishment of Christ's saving mission. In doing so, they have nurtured the pre-

---

[181] Loveland, pg. 175-177.

conditions that have enabled the American infatuation with military power to flourish.

Put another way, were it not for the support offered by several tens of millions of evangelicals, militarism in this deeply and genuinely religious country becomes inconceivable.[182]

In the perspective of the adherents of mainline Christian denominations and evangelicals, America has to resort to military intervention to prove that the Christian God is greater than the enemy, whether it be German Fascism, Japan, communism or the present Islam, even if it needs to destroy their civilian population, culture and civilization in the process. This perspective was fine for OT Israel in defeating the Philistines, but it does not apply to the era of the gospel of the Prince of Peace.

71 THE ROMAN CATHOLIC CHURCH AND GERMAN NATIONAL SOCIALISM

It would be most appropriate to include a chapter on the relationship of Roman Catholicism to National Socialism in Germany and its impact on the European war front and other atrocities during the period 1933-1945. Eugenio Pacelli (1878-1958) rose in the ranks of the Roman Catholic Church (RCC) from priest to Vatican lawyer to archbishop to Cardinal Secretary of State and then to becoming Pope Pius XII. During the years 1930 to 1939, Pacelli, as Cardinal Secretary of State, was the second most powerful person in the RCC next to the pope. His vision during these years was the institution of the RCC as the legal and official religion in countries that had a large Catholic population, regardless of the concessions that would have to be made. It was not without precedence that

---

[182] Bacevich, pg. 140

treaties – or concordats – had been made throughout the centuries between the Vatican and other countries, and they defined the role of the RCC in that country and the responsibility of the state toward the ROC.

The initial concordat concluded by Pacelli was between the Vatican and the country Serbia on June 24, 1914. Members of the RCC acquired freedom of religion, worship and education, while the state of Serbia placed all RCC clergy on its payroll. Concurrently, the Serbian state would be the protector of the Catholic Church and its members in the country.[183] Another concordat of importance was that with Bavaria in March 1924, created by Pacelli and Pope Pius XI, and passed by the Bavarian parliament. Pacelli was able to acquire recognition, protection and advancement of the RCC in Bavaria, as well as the salary of all RCC clergy in the country, provided that only German or Bavarian citizens would be employed in the RCC. Another concordat of similar content was signed with Prussia on June 14, 1929, [184]

The Lateran Treaty was concluded in February 1929, between the papacy and Benito Mussolini and his Fascist Italian government. The treaty was created by Cardinal Secretary of State Pietro Gasparri, Pacelli's predecessor. According to the terms of the Lateran Treaty, the RCC became the sole recognized religion of Italy, but the concession made by the RCC was that all RCC members had to withdraw from politics. This of course allowed fascists to fill the void. RCC clergy were likewise prohibited from being active in any political issue.[185]

Adolf Hitler, during his rise to power, realized the potential for Catholic resistance and that something had to be done to suppress it, because as dictator he could not permit allegiance to any other authority other than himself. It was either National Socialism or the RCC that would have the supremacy of ideology

---

[183] Cornwell, John, *Hitler's Pope: The Secret History of Pius XII*, pg.48-49.
[184] Cornwell, pgg. 100-103.
[185] Cornwell, pg. 114-115.

and authority in Germany, and for Hitler it was going to be him and not the papacy. As historian Cornwell described it:

> Hitler in fact had two views on the churches – public and private. In February of 1933 he was to declare in the Reichstag that the churches were to be an integral part of German national life. Privately, the following month, he vowed to completely "eradicate" Christianity from Germany. "You are either a Christian or a German," he said, "You cannot be both." In the meantime, he was bent on careful manipulation of the power of the churches to his own ends.[186]

What Hitler said in private – his cooperation with the Christian church – was different than what he said in public – its eradication. He then proceeded in the path he felt would be in his best interests: manipulate the RCC to his advantage by limiting their role and responsibility in Germany, in exchange for survival.

In 1930, 35 million Catholics resided in Germany, 1/3 the population of the county. Although a minority, their clergy were more aggressive in opposing the rise of Nazism than the protestant – and mainly Lutheran – clergy. Catholicism in Germany initially waged an ideological war with the Nazi party, but Pacelli was in process of creating his own treaty or concordat with the Reich, a treaty that would increase his power within the institution of the RCC, but render it ineffective in moral and social concerns in Germany.

After hearing of the Lateran Treaty, Hitler hoped for something of the same for Germany. Because of the Nazi ideological war against Judaism, democracy and communism, and its drive to subject Christianity – especially the RCC – to its authority, Pope Pius XI and Pacelli thought in terms of a temporary and tactical compromise with Hitler, the purpose

---

[186] Cornwell, pg. 105-106.

being the survival of the RCC and the authority of the papacy in Germany, as limited as it might be. This alliance with the devil – much like the Lateran Treaty with the fascist Italian government – was the result of the papacy's fears for the future of the RCC as an institution in Germany. Negotiations began for a Reich Concordat with the personal participation of Hitler and Pacelli. As Cromwell described the situation:

> Hitler saw with great clarity that the concordat would be presented as a papal endorsement of the Nazi regime and its policies. Realizing the impatience of Pacelli and the inherent weakness of the Cardinal Secretary's aims, preoccupied as they were with the power of the Holy See, Hitler could dictate the pace of the negotiations and manipulate them entirely to his own considerable advantage.[187]

Even though German RCC bishops were aware that the ideology of National Socialism was diametrically opposite from Christianity, only a minority objected to the terms of the Reich Concordat, and specifically to the article that prohibited them from any type of social action or political activity. The Nazi party, of course, would define what social action and political activity consisted of. Before the concordat was even finalized, Nazi police were already arresting Catholic clergy involved in social and political activities, while others were subjected to a wave of terror. At the same time, due to the rise of the Nazi party in Germany and as a result of patriotism and peer pressure, Catholics were abandoning their religion and joining the Nazis in massive proportions.

On July 8, 1933, the Reich Concordat between the RCC and German government was signed. The RCC placed itself at the mercy and service of the Nazi party in exchanged for its survival as a sacerdotal institution in Germany. The RCC clergy was

---

[187] Cornwell, pg. 143.

reduced to the performance of rites and sacraments, provided that they refuse to become involved in social and political issues, and the Nazi government in trade kept their churches open for services. The ramifications were only obvious. This event effectively emasculated any voice that Catholic clergy might have in Germany to oppose the war or annihilation of Jews and other minority religions and cultures. There was no voice of censure or reprimand from the RCC clergy as Germany proceeded with their unimpeded invasion of other countries, World War 2 in Europe, the annihilation of Jews and other minorities, and the persecution of countless others who refused subjection to the Nazi government. The RCC was reduced to a sacramental duty by the Vatican for the purpose of its survival, and at the expense of the millions that died in the period 1933-1945. The reasons for the capitulation of the RCC to the Nazi German government were very apparent: the papacy could not envision an RCC without churches and cathedrals, without priests and a sacerdotal hierarchy, without rites and traditions, and without ecclesiastical paraphernalia, and especially without the power base of the papacy.

In the narrow worldview of the RCC papacy, Christianity cannot exist except as a political and ecclesiastical institution. As a result, the RCC clergy doomed millions of others to be slaughtered as lambs, rather than passively resisting the Nazi and Fascist governments and be sacrificed themselves. If the RCC clergy took the example of Christ and were willing to be sacrificed as a part of passive resistance, such an action would also have reduced the lives lost during these years. German soldiers and executioners would then take the example of their spiritual leaders, who were willing to die rather than condone or authorize the killing, and so they would have desisted killing and the killing would stop. This course of action would have reduced the RCC as an institution, but the gospel of the Prince of Peace would have continued unassailable.

On March 2, 1939, Eugenio Pacelli was elected pope, becoming Pope Pius XII, and he upheld the terms of both the

Lateran Treaty and Reich Concordat through his term of office.[188] More Catholics died during his papal term than during the term of any other pope in history.

---

[188] Cornwell, pg. 207-209.

PART SEVEN

CHRISTIAN PACIFISM IN AMERICA

I have not come to destroy people's lives, but to save them.
Jesus Christ, Luke 9:56.

72   WILLIAM PENN AND QUAKER PENNSYLVANIA

From 1681 to 1756, for a term of 75 years, Pennsylvania was a pacifist state, and was governed by a Friends' dominated colonial assembly. The drawback that ultimately led to the capitulation to a militarist policy was its administration by a secular governor and the colony's status as a subject of the British Crown.

William Penn's vision and effort was admirable, as he took advantage of a debt owed his father by King Charles II of England to acquire land in America, and primarily the east half of the present-day state of Pennsylvania and Delaware. Penn's vision was a state based on Quaker principles, and primarily, the resolution of all conflicts in a peaceful manner without resorting to violence or war. His initial charter expressed freedom of religious conviction for all residents, and which he was convinced that eventually the "Inner Light" would enlighten every person residing in his colony with Quaker precepts. The Charter was issued March 4, 1681, making him governor and proprietor, and the property was assigned to him and his heirs or assignees for the infinite future, provided they abided by English law and under the ultimate auspices of the English crown. This inclusion would eventually lead the colony to subject itself to the pressure of England during the French and Indian War.

William Penn created several charters for the residents of his colony, of which the following is a passage from the Charter of October 28, 1701, regarding freedom of religion:

> Because no People can be truly happy, though under the greatest Enjoyment of Civil Liberties, if abridged of the Freedom of their Consciences, as to their Religious Profession and Worship: And Almighty God being the only Lord of Conscience, Father of Lights and Spirits; and the Author as well as Object of all divine Knowledge, Faith and Worship, who only doth enlighten the Minds, and persuade and convince the Understandings of People, I do hereby grant and declare, That no Person or Persons, inhabiting in this Province or Territories, who shall confess and acknowledge One almighty God, the Creator, Upholder and Ruler of the World; and profess him or themselves obliged to live quietly under the Civil Government, shall be in any Case molested or prejudiced, in his or their Person or Estate, because of his or their conscientious Persuasion or Practice, nor be compelled to frequent or maintain any religious Worship, Place or Ministry, contrary to his or their Mind, or to do or suffer any other Act or Thing, contrary to their religious Persuasion.

Penn arrived in the New World on November 8, 1682, and with other Friends founded the city of brotherly love, Philadelphia. The Charter's provisions attracted a wide assortment of Christians of every denomination seeking a haven and freedom from persecution in Europe that by 1776, Pennsylvania had some 300,000 population, while Philadelphia had 18,000 residents, America's largest city. The "Holy Experiment" in this respect was an immense success. William Penn did not remain long in Pennsylvania, which was to the disadvantage of the government of the colony to keep it under control of Quaker tenets. Although the colonial assembly was a majority of Friends, and legislative policy was based on Quaker principles, the initial governors were not Quaker and were not at all after about 1710.

The personal tragedy of William Penn made his initial rule – and the subsequent rule of his successors – ineffective. Penn returned to England after only 2 years in America. During his sojourn in England, Penn lost his charter to the Governor-General of New York, Benjamin Fletcher in 1692, but then regained it in 1694, at which time he returned to Pennsylvania. In 1703, Penn returned to England, there to remain. Due to financial difficulties, Penn returned the Charter to the administration of the English Crown in 1711, and suffered a stroke in 1712. He remained with his family until his death July 30, 1718.

The British continued to exact taxes from Pennsylvania, approved by the Quaker-dominated assembly as "for the King's use." Nonetheless, the money was used to build forts and create a militia to guard the colony, especially during the period after Penn's final departure in 1703. Friends were only 20% of the population of Pennsylvania, although they dominated the policy of the colony with their aggressive effort to keep pacifism as a primary tenet. The 80% balance was an indigenous assortment of denominations, some of which were pacifist, while most were not, including Jews.

The defeat of pacifism as a principle tenet of Pennsylvania occurred in 1755-1756 during the French and Indian War. The British government pressured the Friends-dominated colonial assembly to appropriate taxes in November 1755, which were to be used directly in the war of the British against the French. Increased pressure of the British government on the colonial assembly for them to declare war finally succeeded on June 7, 1756, but not without the resignation of 7 prominent Friend assembly members. The tendency of the Friends in the colonial assembly to compromise with war and military service was likewise the indirect result of the majority population of Pennsylvania being militarist orientated. Another factor was the political and economic pressure applied by the state of New York, directly to the north.

The success of the Holy Experiment – as many labeled it – can be measured in the fact that Philadelphia became the seat of representative religious freedom in the US during the 2nd half of the 18th century. The Charters of William Penn also had a direct effect on the inclusion of religious freedom in the First Amendment of the Bill of Rights.[189]

73   CHRISTIAN PACIFISM AND THE CIVIL WAR

The initial bill for Civil War conscription was the Conscription Act passed on March 3, 1863, but the act did not contain any exemptions on religious grounds. On February 24, 1864, the act was revised and included provisions for conscientious objectors.

> That members of religious denominations, who shall by oath of affirmation declare that they are conscientiously opposed to the bearing of arms, and who are prohibited from doing so by the rules and articles of faith and practice of said religious denominations shall, when drafted into the military service, be considered non-combatants, and shall be assigned by the Secretary of War to duty in the hospitals, or to the care of freedmen, or shall pay the sum of three hundred dollars to such persons as the Secretary of War shall designate to receive it, to be applied to the benefit of the sick and wounded soldiers; provided, that no person shall be

---

[189] Brock, Peter, *Pacifism in the United States from the Colonial Era to the First World War*, pgg. 81-158.

entitled to the provisions of this section unless his declaration of conscientious scruples against bearing arms shall be supported by satisfactory evidence that his department has been uniformly consistent with such declaration.

The lone voice of Christian pacifism of this era was Adin Ballou (1803–1890), a Unitarian and Universalist minister in New York and Massachusetts, and a fervent abolitionist and social activist of the middle 19th century. He turned to Christian pacifist in 1838 and continued his effort through the Civil War years.

Ballou's principals for the Christian non-resistant are outlined in the following list:

1. He cannot kill, maim otherwise injure any human being, in personal self-defense, or for the sake of his family or any thing he holds hear;
2. He cannot participate in any lawless conspiracy, mob, riotous assembly, or disorderly combination of individuals, or cause or countenance the commission of any such absolute injury;
3. He cannot be an officer or private, chaplain or retainer in the army, navy or militia of any nation, state or chieftain.
4. He cannot be an officer, elector, agent, legal prosecutor, passive constituent, or approver of any government, as a sworn or otherwise pledged supporter thereof, whose civil constitution and fundamental laws require, authorize or tolerate war, slavery, capital punishment, or the infliction of personal injury.[190]

His effort and books were very influential on the next generation of Christian peace activists in the USA after the Civil War. Leo Tolstoy was also indebted to Adin Ballou in the development of his ideas on Christian pacifism.

---

[190] Ballou, Adin, *Christian Non-Resistance*, pg. 15-16.

Immense suffering were incurred on American soil during the Civil War of 1861-1865: about 620,000 fatalities (over 15% of the total number of soldiers) and the physical and economic devastation of the states that comprised the Confederacy, and an immeasurable quantity of wounded soldiers, as well as the suffering of many innocent northerners and southerners. As a result, after the conclusion of the Civil War, the attitude toward war and preparation for war changed among ecclesiastical leaders. The sermons of the pulpits of every denomination and every congregation began to denounce war and urged politicians to enact peace treatises and to reconcile any possible conflict before it would rupture into conflict and lead to war.

Some 30 peace organizations were created during the period of 1865-1914, and some, as the American Peace Society, which started in 1815, expanded. These groups had impressive titles such as the World Peace Foundation, the Federal Council of the Churches in Christ, and the Carnegie Endowment for International Peace. In January 1914, while Europe was still calm, the Church Peace Union was created with a $2 million endowment from Andrew Carnegie to finance the efforts toward world peace. Many prominent clergy and laymen from Protestant, Catholic and Jewish faith joined the Church Peace Union. With the amount of peace propaganda that was published by these organizations and distributed, and the number of sermons preached on this topic many felt that America was the nation of God to initiate world peace.

From the American Civil War in 1865, there were no major military conflicts until war was declared on Germany in 1917, except for the brief Spanish-American War of 1898.

74   CHRISTIAN PACIFISM AND WORLD WAR ONE

Exemption from military service for conscientious objectors during World War One was permitted by Section 1644 of the Selective Service Law of May 18, 1917, which, in summary, allowed the exemption based on 2 primary conditions. This was codified as Rule XIV of section 79 of the Selective Service Regulations.

> Any registrant who is found by a Local Board to be a member of any well-recognized religious sect or organization organized and existing May 18, 1917, and whose then existing creed or principles forbid its members to participate in war in any form, and whose religious convictions are against war or participation therein in accordance with the creed or principles of said religious organization, shall be furnished by such Local Board with a certificate (Form 1008, sec. 280, p.225) to that effect and to the further effect that, by the terms of Section 4 of the Selective Service Law, he can only be required to serve in a capacity declared by the President to be noncombatant.[191]

Out of 2.8 million who were inducted into the armed forces of the USA during World War I, only almost 4,000 made a claim as conscientious objectors to war, whether on religious or other grounds. Of this number, about 1,300 reevaluated their position and eventually joined the military as soldiers or in noncombatant service. Another 1,500 were sent to work on farms, about 100 were assigned to the Friends Reconstruction Unit (hospital work), while 450 were courts-martialled and sent to prison. The balance of 650 were kept in custody at various military installations near to their home, and were isolated from the balance of the servicemen. The farm furlough was the most desirable means of complying with the state as a conscientious objection. Since the war removed many able-bodied workers from agriculture, many farms were willing to accept COs (conscientious objectors) as laborers.[192]

---

[191] Kellogg, Water Guest, *The Conscientious Objector*, pg. 140, and, Schlissel, Lillian, *Conscience in America*, pg. 133.
[192] Kellog, Walter Guest, *The Conscientious Objector*, pgg. 75-81.

All of these men – as few at there were – did not go unnoticed by mainline denominational preachers, and were heavily discredited. Eventually because of war hysteria all peace movements in America came under suspicion and which turned clergy against the conscientious objector.

> The replies from famous [Episcopal] bishops, some of whom were against any exemption for the COs, classing them as cowards, sentimentalists, and anarchists, indicate that the bishops, in general were uncompromising. One Southern Episcopal bishop said, "The real conscientious objector is unbalanced. True Christian churchmen are dying for Christ."[193]

> James Samuel Stone, rector of St. James Church, Chicago, gave it as his opinion that the pacifist was the most despicable and craven creature that crawls the earth, and that the word pacifist was the most disgraceful word in the English language.[194]

The conscientious objectors came from primarily the smaller denominational peace churches: Mennonites were about 50% of the COs. Jehovah's Witnesses, Dunkards (Brethren), Quakers (Friends), made up an additional 25% of the COs, while the 25% balance were Israelites of the House of David, Seventh-Day Adventists, Pentecostals, Molokans, Christadelphians, Church of Christ, a handful of Catholic, and the balance were from a heterogeneous assortment of lesser denominations, including one Jew.[195]

Regarding those 450 objectors who were courts-martialled, apart from about 100 political objectors, the balance of 350 religious objectors consisted of 138 Mennonites; 27 International Bible Students (Jehovah's Witnesses); 24 Dunkards (Brethren);

---

[193] Abrams, pg. 136.
[194] Abrams, pg. 133.
[195] Abrams, pgg.127-129.

13 Quakers (Friends); 17 Church of God Holiness; 17 Church of Christ; 11 Seventh Day Adventists; 13 Pentecostals; 6 Russian Molokans; 4 Apostolic Faith; 4 House of David; 3 Plymouth Brethren; and 1 Christadelphian; and the balance were independents who either did not associate themselves with any denomination, or were members of mainline denominations that were normally not considered peace churches. Seventeen of them received the death sentence (although it was later commuted), 142 were given life in prison, 73 received 20-year prison terms, while 15 received 3-years or less imprisonment.

The incarcerated objectors were assigned primarily to Fort Jay, Governors Island, NY; Fort Leavenworth, KS (which the US military labeled the Concentration Camp for conscientious objectors);[196] and Alcatraz Island, San Francisco Bay, CA. Every one of these endured critical and barbaric suffering at the hands of prison officials during their period of incarceration, and one, Ernest Gellert from New Jersey, committed suicide on April 8, 1918, unable to suffer both the physical and psychological abuse. At least 17 objectors died while incarcerated as a result of torture or inadequate prisons conditions: Charles W. Bolly, Frank Burde, Reuben J. Eash, Julius Firestone, Daniel B. Flory, Henry E. Franz, Ernest Gellert (suicide), brothers Joseph and Michael Hofer, Hohannes M. Klassen, Van Skedine, Walter Sprunger, Daniel E. Teuscher, Mark R. Thomas, Ernest D. Wells, John Wolfe, and Daniel S. Yoder. Twelve of them were religious objectors, 3 were socialists, with no information about the remaining 2. Most of them died at Leavenworth.[197] In general, the clergy of mainline denominations, as well as government officials, did little or nothing to assist the plight of the suffering COs who were incarcerated or restricted at military installations.

The Espionage Act of June 15, 1917, and its amendment of May 16, 1918, made the arrest and prosecution of peace activists

---

[196] Kohn, Stephen M., *Jailed for Peace, the History of American Draft Law Violators*, pg. 35.
[197] Kohn, pg. 42.

very easy, as well as objectors to military service of every sort. Section 32 of the Act read:

> Whoever ... shall willfully cause or attempt to cause insubordination, disloyalty, mutiny, refusal of duty, in the military or naval forces of the United States, or shall willfully obstruct the recruiting of enlistment service of the United States, to the injury of the service or of the United States, shall be punished by a fine of not more that $10,000 or imprisonment of not more than twenty years, or both.

The typical observer would notice in the above Act the deprivation of freedom of speech, freedom of the press, and freedom of the exercise of ones religion, all in the name of war hysteria. Essentially, if a person did not support the war effort, then that person was aiding and abetting the enemy indirectly by reducing the patriotism of American citizens. As a result, by mid-1918, about 10,000 non-registrants were arrested and prosecuted, and half of those who evaded induction or deserted were apprehended.

Three Christian pacifists: Robert Whitaker, Floyd Hardin, and Harold Storey, were arrested in Los Angeles in September 1917 for voicing their opinion against the militarist trend of Christian denominations. A mob led by businessmen and clergy broke into their meeting and took custody of the three. They were subsequently tried under the provisions of the Espionage Act of 1917, and were convicted. Their sentence was $1500 fine and 6 months incarceration.

Evangelist Billy Sunday was vehement in his denunciation of pacifists:

> The Christian pacifists ought to be treated as Frank Little[198] was at Butte and then let the coroner do the rest.[199]

War hysteria created mob violence against Germans, COs, and any who did not display sufficient patriotism and support for the war. Hundreds of incidences of mob violence are recorded, occurring in cities large and small throughout the continental USA. Numerous lynching occurred of ministers who opposed conscription, while other anti-war protesters were tarred and feathered. Yellow paint was applied to homes of person suspected of anti-war propaganda or for not participating in war loan drives.[200]

After the Armistice of November 11, 1918, the incarcerated religious objectors were released from prison, but at a trickle. Few mainline denominational clergy exerted the effort for their release, and their freedom was dependant on the whim of the War Department. The task for the resolution of the incarcerated COs was assigned to Walter Guest Kellogg, Major Judge Advocate, US Army, and eventually all were released by November 1920.

---

[198] Frank Little is an example of a victim of war hysteria and graft during World War 1. He was a union organizer for the Industrial Workers of the World (IWW), and concentrated his efforts on organizing miners in Montana and Arizona. Little was a proponent of free speech and developed the union tactic of nonviolent resistance. He was feared by Anaconda Copper of Montana due to his union organization efforts at their copper mine near Butte, MT. With WW1 under way, copper was a valuable commodity with Anaconda reaping much profit with high prices and the low wages of its mine workers.

When WW1 broke out, Little was vociferous in his opposition to American entrance into it, and combined his anti-war rhetoric with his union organization, informing members of the IWW not to join the military. As a result of such campaigns, and the IWW already suspected of being a socialist front, Little was suspected by the US government of being a traitor to American patriotism. On August 1, 1917, 6 men broke into Little's hotel room in Butte, MT, beat him up, tied him to the car and dragged him through the streets. He was then lynched at a trestle outside of town and his body was left to hang over the railroad tracks.

No one was ever arrested or prosecuted for Little's murder, although many felt it was a combination of FBI and Anaconda Copper anti-union officials who bribed some local over-zealous patriotic thugs.

[199] Abrams, pgg. 216-217

[200] Abrams, pgg. 216-217.

75 CHRISTIAN PACIFISM AND WORLD WAR TWO

Congress passed the Selective Training and Service Act on September 14, 1940, and it was signed into law by President Roosevelt 2 days later. Section 5(g) of the act, which deal with conscientious objectors to military service, read as follows:

> Nothing contained in this act shall be construed to require any person to be subject to combatant training and service in land and naval forces of the United States who, by reason of religious training and belief, is conscientiously opposed to participation in war in any form. Any such person claiming such exemption from combatant training and service because of such conscientious objections, whose claim is sustained by the local draft board, shall, if he is inducted into the land or naval forces under this Act, be assigned to noncombatant service as defined by the President or shall, if he is found to be conscientiously opposed to participation in such noncombatant service, in lieu of such induction, be assigned to work of national importance under civilian direction.

Of the 34.5 million men who registered for the draft during WW2, 72,354 applied as COs. Of these, 25,000 accepted noncombatant service in the armed forces, while another 27,000 failed the medical examination. About 12,000 accepted the alternative program of civilian public service, while 6,100 were incarcerated.

As a result of maltreatment of COs during WW1, and once Germany began preparations for possible war in Europe, the historic peace churches of the USA began a cooperative effort to determine some type of resolution for the CO should the USA go to war again. They did not want the same unnecessary persecution to reoccur as a result of war hysteria. The leaders of the peace churches expected a flood of COs to refuse conscription as a result of the massive peace efforts by mainline denominations during the decade of the 1920s and early 1930s. But their fears quickly dissipated. Just as the vocal peace movements of 1910-1917 changed course once America declared war on Germany, the same occurred after the Japanese attack on Pearl Harbor: the peace movements again changed their course, and so there were considerably less COs for the peace churches to deal with than they originally anticipated.

A three-person committee was formed in October 1935 to propose a solution to the Selective Service System regarding COs, should the USA go to war. The men were: Orie Miller, a Mennonite; C. Ray Kein, a Brethren (Dunkard); and Robert Balderston, a Friend (Quaker). After several more meetings the consensus was alternative humanitarian service as civilians, without compensation from the US government. The alternative service would be under civilian control, regulated and financed by the historic peace churches, and would not include any work that would be associated with the war effort.

It was primarily through the efforts of Paul C. French that the provisions for COs and the definition of a CO (conscientious objector) was presented in its final form, submitted to Congress, and approved. The specific clause, "by way of religious training and belief," in the new version of the exemption for COs, replaced the clause of the WW1 exemption, where membership in a historic peace church was a requirement. This now allowed any person of any denomination who was a CO to acquire an exemption, and which had been very difficult during WW1 if a person was not a member of a historic peace church.

Col. Lewis B. Hershey, who joined the Selective Service System on October 1, 1940 – and directed the department until his retirement in April 1973 – requested Paul French to make arrangement for the peace churches to direct the CPS program for COs. Executive order 8675 (6 FR 831) was signed by President Roosevelt on February 6, 1941, and read as follows:

Authorizing the Director of Selective Service To Establish or Designate Work of National Importance Under Civilian Direction for Persons Conscientiously Opposed to Combatant and Non-Combatant Service in the Land or Naval Forces of the United States.

The program became known as Civilian Public Service – CPS – but was still under the administration of the Selective Service System. For Hershey, who whole-heartedly supported the CPS program, it was a means of removing the CO from public view and from military installations, thus eliminating them as a detriment to conscription or the war effort in general: out of sight, out of mind.

The CPS program lasted from May 1941 to April 1947, with some 9,000 COs participating in the program at 152 camps (the other 3,000 served time as medical attendants in hospitals and mental institutions). The actual assignment of COs to the camps was made by the Selective Service. The definition of "work of national importance" was vague, but inevitably ended up meaning either forestry or hospital related work. The CPS camps were for the most part obsolete Civilian Conservation Corp camps that were established by the US government during depression era to put unemployed civilians to work. They were then converted for use by the CPS program.[201]

Members of over 200 Christian denominations who acquired an exemption from military service as COs were assigned to alternative service within the CPS program, including 10 Jews. About 60% were from the historic peace churches (Mennonite, Friends, Brethren); about 15 % were from mainline denominations; another 15% were from smaller denominations, while the balance were independents without denominations affiliation.[202]

---

[201] The author's father was assigned to Three Rivers CPS camp, near Visalia, CA, in the lower Sierra Mountains.
[202] Keim, Albert N., *The CPS Story*, pg. 80.

The CPSers worked at an immense variety of projects, including conservation and forestry camps, hospitals and training schools, university labs, agricultural experiment stations and farms, and as government survey crews. They built roads, fought forest fires, constructed dams, planted trees, built contour strips on farms, served as guinea pigs for medical and scientific research, built sanitary facilities for hookworm-ridden communities and cared for the mentally ill and juvenile delinquents.[203]

COs were not lax in their assignments, and especially made improvements at mental health facilities. COs as hospital orderlies provided better care for the patients than did the regular employees, and reforms were implemented as a result of their contributions. Over the 6-year CPS program, COs contributed over 8 million man-days of work at no expense to the US government (at about a $22 million value at the time in equivalent wages), but with the contribution of $7 million by the historic peace churches and the families and churches of the other CPS participants. The cost to the US government in administrative expenses was about $4.7 million.[204]

The incarcerated COs suffered immensely, but not to the extent of those during WW1, now with the Selective Service System having improved conditions for their incarceration. These COs served time in federal prisons, and not in military jails or at military installations, the most prominent being Terminal Island Penitentiary, CA, McNeil Island Penitentiary, WA, Tucson Federal Penitentiary, Tucson, AZ, Danbury Federal Penitentiary, CT, Federal Correctional Institution of Texarkana, TX, Milan Federal Correctional Institutional, MI, Ashland Federal Correctional Institution, KY, Tucson Federal

---

[203] Keim, pg. 40.
[204] Keim, pg. 40.

Correctional Institution, AZ, and Lewisburg Federal Penitentiary, PA.

On December 25, 1944, for example, at the Federal Road Camp #10, Tucson, AZ, 200 Jehovah's Witnesses and 60 COs from other denominations, plus 5 Russian Molokan COs, were incarcerated. In addition to them were 31 Japanese-Americans and 5 Hopi Indians, who were also arrested, tried and sentenced as Selective Service law violators for refusing conscription. The Japanese-Americans who refused conscription felt that their civil rights were being violated.[205] Stephen Kohn in his book on CO inmates of WW2 mentions the following:

> Conscientious objectors suffered the deprivations and abuses of prison life. They faced strict prison routine, isolation or solitary confinement for punishment, a poor diet, boredom, and loneliness. Despite the official policy against torture, a number of abuse cases were reported. At McNeil Island Federal Prison, a CO reported being beaten by guards. Other objectors were punished by denial of food, withholding of medicine... In another prison a Molokan religious objector was placed in solitary confinement for 111 days and beaten semi-conscious for refusing to stop discussing the Bible with fellow inmates.[206]

Fortunately, the maximum sentence for refusing induction was 5 years, while the average length of actual incarceration was 35 months. Most of the inmates were released by October 1946, about 1-1/2 years after the end of the war, while others persisted in prison or CPS camps until mid-1947. However, it was not until President Harry Truman issued a Proclamation of Amnesty on December 23, 1947 (Proclamation 2762), that a pardon was

---

[205] Cantine, Holly, and Rainer, Dachine, *Prison Etiquette*, pg. 80.
[206] Kohn, pgg. 52-53.

extended toward all violators of the draft law, except for the Jehovah Witnesses.[207]

76   CHRISTIAN PACIFISM AND THE VIETNAM WAR

Unlike the "war to make the world safe for democracy," or the "good war," the Vietnam War was regularly opposed by many American Christian denominations. Perhaps not all at the beginning of the war, but eventually most of them issued statements at one time or another to stop the bombing of North Vietnam and to withdraw troops as casualties increased. Several of the mainline denominations that were historical militarist also had departments that provided information on conscientious objection to military service and assistance to acquire a CO exemption. These denominations included the Catholic Church, American Lutheran Church, American Baptist Church, Methodist Church, United Church of Christ, Episcopal Church, and the United Presbyterian Church. Thousands of members of the CALCAV[208] demonstrated against the bombing of Vietnam in the front of the White House on January 31, 1967.[209]

The criteria for an exemption as a conscientious objector during Vietnam read as follows in the Selective Service Regulations:[210]

(a) A registrant must be conscientiously opposed to participation in war in any form and conscientiously opposed to participation in both combatant and noncombatant training and service in the Armed Forces.

---

[207] 12 FR 8731 (3 CFR, 1943-1948 Comp., p. 145.); Schlissel, Lillian, *Conscience in America*, pg. 217
[208] Clergy and Laymen concerned about Vietnam
[209] Zaroulis, Nancy, and Sullivan, Gerald, *Who Spoke Up? American Protest against the War in Vietnam 1963-1975*. pg. 102.
[210] 32 CFR XVI, par. 1636.4 (Basis for classification in class 1-O)

(b) A registrant's objection may be founded on religious training and belief; it may be based on strictly religious beliefs, or on personal beliefs that are purely ethical or moral in source or content and occupy in the life of a registrant a place parallel to that filled by belief in a Supreme Being for those holding more traditionally religious view.
(c) A registrant's objection must be sincere.

From 1952 to 1964, during the era between the Korean and Vietnam Wars, 85% of all COs were from the historic peace churches (Mennonite, Friends, Brethren), while mainline denominations[211] only supplied 2.6%, and the balance were from smaller evangelical or non-mainline groups, or those who claimed no affiliation. Once the Vietnam War was progressing and conscription was legislated, by 1969, the peace churches only provided 50% of the COs, and mainline denominations provided 27%, while 10% claimed no affiliation (24,000 COs compared to 262,000 inductions). The following year, 1970, the peace churches provided 40%, while mainline denominations provided 30%, and now 20% claimed no affiliation (39,000 COs compared to 203,000 inductions). Jehovah's Witnesses were also a considerable proportion but they fall into the "non-mainline" group category, and little data is available regarding them, except as noted below as absolutists.[212] As the war progressed more and more military-age Americans applied for and received CO exemptions. In 1970, 25% of all those who received induction notices became COs; in 1971, the proportion increased to 42%; while in 1972, more young men received exemptions as COs than were recruited into the military. In December 1972, President Nixon realized that forced conscription had failed and ended the maneuver.

---

[211] These are the Catholic, Methodist, Episcopalian, Presbyterian, Unitarian, United Church of Christ, Lutheran, Baptist, and Jewish.
[212] Nelson, Karl D, *By Reason of Religious Training and Belief.*

But not all religious objectors that applied for a CO exemption received one. The number that ignored their receipt of conscription notices were 14,422 in the spring of 1967, while by the spring of 1969, the number rose to 23,280, but very few were actually prosecuted. Most went underground and some who were apprehended migrated to Canada while their case was pending. During the entire period of 1964-1975, a total of 8,756 were indicted for Selective Service law violations; but only 4,001 of were actually tried in Federal Courts, sentenced and incarcerated. Their average term of imprisonment was 32 months. On the average, 7% were from the historic peace churches; 72% of them were from other denominations or were non-religious; and 21% were Jehovah's Witnesses.[213]

As an example, on June 30, 1968, 739 men were held in US prisons as violators of the Selective Service laws. Of them, 574 were Jehovah's Witnesses; 62 were from the historic peace churches; and the rest were from other denominations, including a few Black Muslims. Willard Gaylin, MD, a psychologist, visited several Vietnam War-era COs in various prisons and recorded the following:

> Prisons are not designed for men like them and therefore they are not afforded the opportunities – those limited opportunities – that other prisoners are offered. However, in addition to the de facto discrimination there is actual discrimination. They are not allowed involvement in work-release programs. They are not given jobs commensurate with their abilities even when these are available. Their mail is general more heavily censored. And most important, they are excluded from the normal standards for parole consideration.[214]

---

[213] Kohn, Stephen, *Jailed for Peace*, pg. 92-93.
[214] Gaylin, Willard, *In the Service of their Country: War Resistors in Prison*, pg. 330-331.

The majority of effective Vietnam War protest and promotion of conscientious objection came primarily from secular groups, rather than those affiliated with any Christian denomination, and most of these groups were socialist-oriented, or else were an offshoot that separated from their denomination. Mainline churches could only issue diluted statements, such as the Methodist example above, because of their close association with the state. Independent secular groups did not have to worry about symbiotic relationships with state and military officials, which existed with mainline denominations. Such groups were the War Resistors League, Fellowship of Reconciliation, and the National Peace Action Coalition.

Those who claimed to believe in Jesus Christ as the Prince of Peace and claimed to be disciples of his teachings – the mainline and evangelical denominations – were not following his will in preaching the essence of his gospel of peace, while these secular groups filled that void. Those counseling centers that were associated with the historic peace churches, such as the NISBCO (National Inter-Religious Service Board for Conscientious Objectors), CCCO (Central Committee for Conscientious Objectors) and the AFSC (American Friends Service Committee), did fulfill the role that was expected of them by promoting conscientious objection as the only manner that a disciple of Jesus Christ should conduct himself.

PART EIGHT

THE DILEMMA OF MILITARIST CHRISTENDOM

Army chaplains have a dual role as religious leaders and staff officers. Their duties are prescribed by law, DOD policy, Army regulations, religious requirements, and Army mission.
Army Regulation AR 165-1, par. 4-1(b)

77 THE CONCEPT AND PURPOSE OF A MILITARY

The earthly or secular governments are the kingdoms of this world. These are America and the members of the United Nations, and other sovereign states that are politically independent. The power in each of these secular governments is held by a minority of the population, namely the political and military leadership, those who control the financial institutions of the state, and the industrial giants. There exists both a benefit and a detriment in the institution of secular government.

The detriment of secular government lies in the formation of a military along with the massive industrial complex required to support the military. A military is an important facet of the identity and political independence of the nation because it symbolizes the establishment of a sovereign state and which will defend its existence as a corporate entity. The military is thus designed to serve in the best interests of the state as defined by the ruling party, and to violently defend the ideals that the state represents.

War readily and regularly occurs between the nations because it is a self-imposed judgment upon them for their inability to live in peaceful coexistence. Leaders sense power in devising and creating and employing war. A declaration of war is the product of the military regime to justify its development, its preparations, its manufacture of weapons. War benefits the political and military leadership and the industrial giants and financial institutions, while to the detriment of individuals, society and civilization.

The state includes a Selective Service System to keep track of military age Americans for possible recruitment, and has recruitment offices staffed in offices throughout the nation. The enlisted soldier must be taught military science and politics in schools, trained for military service by superiors, clothed with several sets of uniforms and fatigues, fed daily and housed in barracks on military bases. If he is married there is additional allowance for wife and offspring.

A military demands financial support for its existence. The military budget has a voracious and insatiable appetite and causes a financial burden on the average American worker and a debt for the country itself. The reader will understand the expense of war and a standing army by following the career of a military recruit from enlistment to entombment. The weapons he uses must be contracted for, designed, manufactured, tested, and distributed, and the soldiers must be trained in their use. This applies to guns and ammunition, aircraft, missiles, bombs, artillery, ships and submarines; military bases and equipment to operate the bases. Every congressional district in America has a military base of some sort in its locale, to route federal funds unto the area and promote the local economy. Military personal must be transported to the area of warfare. If killed in battle, his body is returned to relatives and buried at the expense of the government. If he survives and acquires an honorable discharge, he is qualified to obtain benefits from the government throughout his life. The expenses of the military never end.

As political philosopher Ayn Rand stated:

> The actual war profiteers of all mixed economies were and are of that type: men with political pull who acquire fortunes by government favor, during or after a war – fortunes which they could not have acquired on a free market.[215]

The development of industry to support the military as a means of boosting the national economy is artificial, because it is not genuinely productive for the material advancement of the population. The attitude of the state is that military production and recruits are expendable and renewable. But for the military-industrial complex, there is money to be made in war.

78   THE VOCATION OF THE SOLDIER

Soldiers are to kill. Make no doubt about it, the purpose of a soldier in the military is to kill the enemy, whether with a knife or bayonet, gun or rifle or machine gun, shooting a missile or dropping a bomb. The soldier only fulfills his obligation when he kills or destroys property belonging to the enemy in a foreign land. Wars are won only by killing more of the enemy and destroying more of their property, than they destroy of you and your property. Wars are fought to be won, not to be lost. A soldier is not in the military to give his life for his country, but to make sure that the enemy gives up his life for his country, and as many that he can kill without losing his own life in the process. All others that are members of the military have the responsibility to assist the soldier in valiantly performing his task, whether giving him the orders to kill and destroy, supplying him with the

---

[215] Rand, Ayn, *Capitalism, The Unknown Ideal*, pg. 40

weapons or equipment necessary to perform this task, tending to his wounds if he is wounded, or by comforting and encouraging him when he loses courage. Whether combatant or non-combatant they are all employees of the state killing industry. If a recruit is killed, the state will acquire another one to replace him, just as it recruited him. All the branches of the military have the common purpose of killing enemies and destroying their property, although each uses a different tactic. General George C. Patton described the expected actions of soldiers just prior to the invasion of Europe in the following manner, in England on May 31, 1944

> "Now I want you to remember that no bastard ever won a war by dying for his country. You win it by making the other poor dumb bastard die for his country.
>
> "My God, I actually pity those poor bastards we're going up against. My God, I do. We're not just going to shoot the bastards, we're going to cut out their living guts and use them to grease the treads of our tanks. We're going to murder those lousy Hun bastards by the bushel. Now some of you boys, I know, are wondering whether or not you'll chicken out under fire. Don't worry about it. I can assure you that you'll all do your duty. The Nazis are the enemy. Wade into them. Spill their blood, shoot them in the belly. When you put your hand into a bunch of goo, that a moment before was your best friend's face, you'll know what to do."

Leo Tolstoy reflects on the role of the soldier based on his military service in the Crimean war by using Andrei Bolkonski as his mouth-piece to his friend Pierre Bezukhov in his novel *War and Peace,* on the eve of the battle at Borodino:

> "War is not courtesy, but the most horrible thing in life; and we ought to understand that and not play at war. As it is now, war is the favorite pastime of the idle and

frivolous. The military calling is the most highly honored.

"But what is war? What is needed for success in warfare? What are the morality of the military? The goal of war is murder; the weapons of war are spying, treachery, and their encouragement, the annihilation of a country's residents, pillaging them or stealing to provide the army's provision, and fraud and falsehood are termed military strategy. The morality of the military class is the absence of freedom, that is, discipline, idleness, ignorance, cruelty, depravity, and drunkenness. And in spite of all this it is the highest vocation, respected by everyone. All the kings... wear military uniforms, and he who kills the most people receives the highest reward.

"They will meet, as we will meet tomorrow, to murder one another; they will kill and maim tens of thousands, and then have thanksgiving services for having killed so many people – whose number is even exaggerated – and they announce a victory, supposing that the more people killed is the greater the achievement."[216]

There is no justification to armed conflict, regardless of the arguments that appear humanitarian and those that claim that force is inevitable to defeat a totalitarian dictator or curb atrocities committed by some regime. Jesus said, "And when you hear of wars and rumors of wars, do not be alarmed; this must take place, but the end is not near." Mark 13:7. He was absolutely right. Armed military conflict has existed from the initial stages of civilization and news of them travels to other areas rapidly. History contains a continuous and uninterrupted vein of turmoil and armed conflict, and any war initiated will run its course until the judgment of God be accomplished. War

---

[216] Tolstoy, Leo, *War and Peace*, Volume 3, Part 2, chapter 25. (My own translation)

has progressed generation after generation in Christian countries because the Christian Church as an institution has failed in its obligation to its founder Jesus Christ.

The typical person incurs sufficient difficulties during the normal course of life without having to seek and create more. Every person succumbs to illness, accidents, work exhaustion, and eventually our own natural death; weather related calamities and natural catastrophes likewise destroy our property and curb our prosperity. War, however, is man-made and does more damage to human progress than does the elements of nature. There is no justifiable reason to increase the difficulties a person will naturally incur by creating war and imposing its destructive effects on themselves and other people and property.

There will never be a war to end war. A person proceeding to battle convinced he will institute peace will not terminate war, but will only contribute to and continue the incessant history of warfare and the manufacture of weapons and military equipment. After the conclusion of one conflict another will arise shortly after in another region and between other nations. War has not been able to accomplish any of its intents or purposes without the mass destruction of property, life and civilization. No war is ever won, it is defeating for all parties involved.

79 THE INEFFICIENCY OF THE MILITARY

Killing is an action that is repulsive to created humans, against the grain of human nature, and all people – except for a small number of psychopathic homicidal maniacs – go through life avoiding the situation of ever having to kill someone. The God-given nature of every person is not to kill, injure or maim or destroy property, and because of this, a great burden is placed on military leaders to make war effective. In order to fight and win wars, the military must alter that God-given nature through indoctrination, training in the use and performance of weapons, and through simulated techniques of killing. Because of this every recruit must undergo a mass metamorphosis in order to be trained to kill and be able to do so on command by his officer without affecting his conscience. This is the reason for the military to require every recruit to successfully pass boot camp training, in order to change or obliterate the inherent repulsion toward killing. All the superficial embellishments of the military attempt to impose on an individual that the vocation of a soldier is honorable: uniforms, insignia, parades, ranks, metals, and benefits. But this is all superficial, because the vocation of a soldier is not honorable. As Lt. Col. Dave Grossman, psychology and military science professor stated:

> The soldier who does kill must overcome that part of him that says he is a murderer of women and children, a foul beast who has done the unforgivable. He must deny the guilt within him, and he must assure himself that the world is not mad, that his victims are less than animals, and they are evil vermin, and that what his nation and his leaders have told him to do is right.
>
> He must believe that not only is this atrocity right, but it is proof that he is morally, socially, and culturally superior to those whom he has killed.... And the killer must violently suppress any dissonant thought that he has done anything wrong. Further, he must violently attack anyone or anything that would threaten his beliefs. His mental health is totally invested in believing that what he has done is good and right.[217]

Because killing is against the grain of human nature, it is very common for soldiers to avoid personal combat, to refrain from discharging their weapons, or shoot away from their target in a direction that would not cause injury or death to an enemy

---

[217] Grossman, Dave, *On Killing: The Psychological Cost of Learning to Kill in War and Society*, pg.209-210.

combatant. During the American Civil War it was the artillery that inflicted most of the casualties, because soldiers in combat deliberately avoided firing their weapons, lest they actually strike someone. Joanna Bourke estimated that during World War I, only 10% of the soldiers were voluntarily courageous or valiant. Each side restrained themselves from shooting and personal combat.[218] (This is the reason why WWI extended for such a long period of time.) During World War II, Colonel S.L.A. Marshall of the US Army interviewed soldiers and concluded, that less than 15% of the infantry actually fired at enemy positions or persons, even though at least 80% had the opportunity to do so. The others either did not fire their weapons or fired indiscriminately, avoiding the possibility of death or injury.[219]

Grossman's estimates are similar. He states that during the Civil War, only 50% of the soldiers fired their weapons, and only a minute percentage of them actually tried to kill an enemy combatant. In WW2 only 15 to 20% of soldiers fired their weapons, while the proportion rose to 50% in the Korean War, and in Vietnam 90% of the soldiers fired their weapons. In another respect though, 40,000 rounds of ammunition – bullets – were expended for every enemy combatant that was killed by an American soldier in the Vietnam War. The repulsion toward killing was also prevalent in pilots. During WW2, only 1% of fighter pilots accounted for 40% of all enemy aircraft that was shot down.[220]

Military research proved that the further the distance the soldier from his target, the higher the efficiency of killing, because the guilt is decreased proportionately to the distance. Since artillery is distant from personal combat, less guilt is felt by soldiers manning such weapons. The same applied to airplanes dropping bombs: the crew is distant and alien from the devastation being caused on the ground.

---

[218] Bourke, Joanna, *An Intimate History of Killing*, pg. 61.
[219] Bourke, ibid, pg. 63.
[220] Grossman, ibid, pg. 109.

Killing is traumatic and psychologically devastating, which makes it objectionable to the average human. It is very typical for soldiers returning from battle to suffer serious psychological problems as a result of the fact that they have killed on the battlefield, from the impact of risking their own life in armed combat, and from watching others die. A World War 2 study indicated that after 60 days of continual battle exposure, 98% of the survivors had permanent psychiatric scars.[221] Even though alcohol and drugs were utilized by soldiers to suppress their emotional devastation at killing and the carnage in the Vietnam War, eventually the trauma would surface. At least 500,000, and as high as 1.5 million, Vietnam War veterans suffered Post-Traumatic Stress Disorder (PTSD). This would be between 18 and 54% of the 2.8 million active combat personnel who served in the Vietnam War, and which produced more psychiatric casualties than any other war in American history.[222] Even at the present, many veterans of the Iraq War suffer from PTSD, with a very high suicide rate among active soldiers.

One war correspondent stated the following after covering many battles, "No one ever charges into battle for God and country." During the war in Kuwait, he quoted a Marine Corps lieutenant colonel as saying, "Just remember, that none of these boys is fighting for home, for the flag, for all that crap the politicians feed the public. They are fighting for each other, just for each other."[223] Survival rather than victory was the primary concern of most soldiers.

One conclusion made by a researcher into the success of military intelligence and strategy concluded the following:

> The Greeks consulted oracles. The Romans tried to read the entrails of sacrificed chickens. Soothsayers, magicians, and charlatans of every kind have long purported to tell rulers how the next war would come

---

[221] Grossman, ibid, pg. 44.
[222] Grossman, ibid, pg. 282.
[223] Hedges, Chris, *War is a Force that Gives us Meaning*, pg.38.

out – for a price. In our time this hoary head wears the "uniform of the day": the computer scientist's white coat. Today's soothsayers are at least as expensive as Roman chickenologists – and about as accurate.[224]

In ancient times, military leaders would consult the local pagan priest or shaman regarding the success of some campaign. The priest would butcher a chicken, view the kidney or liver, and inform the leader of his prognostication. Of course, the reply was as vague as possible and often what the leader wanted to hear. The present military strategists or sources of military information are no more reliable or accurate than that of previous ages, although more sophisticated methods are now used to determine the outcome of a battle.

80 PSYCHOLOGICAL CONTROL OF THE AMERICAN MIND

There are 2 primary methods used by the state to gain psychological control of the American mind: the first is patriotism, the second is reducing the enemy to a sub-human level.

Patriotism is intended to generate a sense of obligation to the nation an individual is a resident of, as a result of providing that person with the privilege of residing there, and the privilege of life, liberty and the pursuit of happiness. Patriotism is intended to impress upon a person the obligation of reimbursement to the government for these privileges through personal sacrifice. Patriotism is instilled into the population beginning with the Pledge of Allegiance to the American flag. This insignia symbolizes the nation as a corporate entity, and for many it is even a religious symbol. Patriotism is also instilled into the American public with national holidays of a political nature and the parades and celebrations on these days, along with the

---

[224] Codevilla, Angelo, *War: Ends and Means*, Pg 67

national celebration of the birthdays of prominent presidents. Patriotism in America is strong, and so strong that refusing to recite the pledge of allegiance can label a person as anti-American, Communist, and undeserving of living in America. The Christian must be aware that although the decision to join the military and fight in armed combat is admired by the general population, and to give your life for your country is considered heroic, and such individuals are awarded medals and honor, it is not the religion of Jesus.

In every war the phenomena arises of portraying the enemy as sub-human. Foreign nationalities are caricatured in the media and by the state as having features that reduce them to the level of animals or barbarians with a Neanderthal mentality. The national enemy is often referred to by discrediting and disgusting terms. By using this psychological maneuver to equate the enemy with an animal, their mass murder or destruction of their civilization becomes equated with the slaughter of animals. During World War II, Germans were Krauts, and the Japanese were Japs. During Vietnam, the Viet-Cong were gooks. The state is very subtle in its ability to convince the mind of the soldier that the enemy is not a human just like himself. As Lt. Col. Dave Grossman stated:

> Killing is what war is all about, and killing in combat, by its very nature, causes deep wounds of pain and guilt. The language of war helps us to deny what war is really about, and in doing so it makes war more palatable.[225]

Euphemisms are equally applied by the military to soften the harsh language that pertains to war: a bullet is a round and a death is a casualty, while the death or injury of innocent or non-military persons is collateral damage.

---

[225] Grossman, ibid, pg. 93.

81   MILITARY ENLISTMENT AND CONSCRIPTION

Once an individual signs enlistment documents and pledges to uphold the constitution of the United States of American, his and her confession as a Christian terminates, because they have subjected themselves and swore obedience to another supreme authority: the secular state, and have denied in the process the Kingdom of God. The following is the oath taken by every person that enters the US armed forces, which is likewise recited by members of the US Chaplaincy.

> I, (name,) do solemnly swear (or affirm) that I will support and defend the Constitution of the United States against all enemies, foreign and domestic; that I will bear true faith and allegiance to the same; and that I will obey the orders of the President of the United States and the orders of the officers appointed over me, according the regulations and the Uniform Code of Military Justice. So help me God.[226]

The ultimate allegiance for any member of the military is the state, not to Jesus. His position of King of Kings or Son of God is recognized only as a matter of personal conviction, but in no way is it allowed to interfere with the state as supreme authority. The military likewise does not permit another set of moral standards for the recruit, and also defines the extent of religious freedom that is permitted. There is no room for a person to have allegiance to God in the armed forces, because this interferes with the ultimate supreme authority of the state, as indicated in the above oath.

Conscription – or the military draft – is the state forcing a person to place himself in harms way – possibly to be killed – and is a violation of the most fundamental premise of the Declaration of Independence, that men are "endowed by their

---

[226] Department of Defense form 4, page 2, *Enlistment Contract*

Creator with unalienable rights, that among these are life, liberty and the pursuit of happiness." Conscription is dictatorial, and antithesis to a free society, because it deprives the citizen of his guaranteed unalienable rights.

Ayn Rand, a political philosopher, wrote during the era of conscription of the Vietnam War:

> Politically, the draft is clearly unconstitutional. No amount of rationalization, neither by the Supreme Count, nor by private individuals, can alter the fact that it represents "involuntary servitude."[227]
>
> Of all the statist violations of individual rights in a mixed economy, the military draft is the worst. It is an abrogation of rights. It negates man's fundamental right – the right to life – and establishes the fundamental principle of statism: that a man's life belongs to the state, and the state may claim it by compelling him to sacrifice it in battle.
>
> If the state may force a man to risk death or hideous maiming and crippling, in a war declared at the state's discretion, for a cause he may neither approve of nor even understand, if his consent is not required to send him into unspeakable martyrdom – then, in principle, all rights are negated in that state, and its government is not man's protector any longer.[228]

In another respect, and this was the lesson learned from Vietnam, conscription is the state's admission of defeat in war. If the state needs to force someone to kill or die for his country, the war is already lost.

One war resister from Boston who was convicted for refusing conscription in 1968 and was sentenced to prison provided his

---

[227] Rand, Ayn, *Capitalism, The Unknown Ideal*, pg. 227
[228] Rand, Ayn, *Capitalism, The Unknown Ideal*, pg. 226-227

view of conscription in the following manner during an interview in prison:

> "I believe that the draft denies the man his right to life. You take a man and put his life on the line, and you control him, lock, stock and barrel. You deprive him of his right to exist. They can push my body around the way they do in prison, but no one is going to force my mind. They are not going to teach me to repair rifles and teach me to shoot it at another person."[229]

Those that are conscripted for the task or war will exert the least amount of effort, or defy the state, as a vendetta for conscription against their will. One example is the inefficiency of the military, discussed above. For people to submit to conscription, the punishment must be severe enough in order for them to submit to conscription rather than try to evade it, such as 5 years imprisonment and $25,000 fine. To insure the effectiveness of the punishment for Selective Service law violation, the state will prosecute a few recalcitrant as sacrifices, as an example to the balance. Impressments into service can now be guaranteed, as men will take the risk of warfare survival, rather than incarceration and its risks. In this manner, the state will always have access to recruits in order to perpetually conduct the business of war.[230]

82   THE CONSTITUTIONALITY OF CONSCRIPTION

The initial judicial decision regarding the constitutionality of conscription dealt with the Conscription Act of 1863 in the suit of Kneedler v. Lane, 45 Pa. St. 238 (1863) in the Pennsylvania Supreme Court.[231] The complaint was filed by Kneedler and

---

[229] Gaylin, Dr. Willard, *In the Service of their Country, War Resisters in Prison*, pg. 278.
[230] Gaylin, ibid, pg. 276.

others against the Enrollment (draft) Board, to restrain them from committing a tort against their persons, being the invasion of their personal liberty and forcing them to submit to conscription against their free will.

Three of the 5 judges at the first hearing held the opinion that the Conscription Act was unconstitutional. Chief Justice Lowrie wrote on November 9, 1863 the majority opinion, stating that the federal government's military recruitment program should be limited to volunteer enlistments in the regular army and requests from the state militia, and should not implement direct conscription. The decision of the judges was split along party lines: 3 Democrat versus 2 Republican judges. Lincoln's administration was desperate for a victory in the Pennsylvania Supreme Court, afraid that the matter would eventually reach the US Supreme Court. Lincoln was aware that Chief Justice Roger Brooke Taney of the US Supreme Court opposed conscription and was eager to declare it unconstitutional. Brooke, a Democrat, was opposed to many activities of Lincoln's Republican administration, and did not consider that the authority of the Federal government to raise an army included conscription.[232]

After the retirement of Justice Lowrie, the Attorney-General of the United States requested a second hearing on December 12, 1863. The new Court heard the arguments and subsequently reversed the initial decision on January 16, 1864, and again the decision was split along party lines: 3 Republican versus 2 Democratic judges. The majority opinion was related by the new Chief Justice Woodward of the Pennsylvania Supreme Court, and the Conscription Act of 1863 was held to be constitutional.[233] The matter was laid to rest after the second hearing and decision of the Pennsylvania Supreme Court until World War 1.

---

[231] Duggan, Joseph, *The Legislative and Statutory Development of the Federal Concept of Conscription for Military Service*, 1946. pgg. 122-123.
[232] Chambers, John Whiteclay III, *To Raise an Army*, pgg. 55-56
[233] Chambers, pgg. 56-57.

America's entrance into World War I occurred when Congress declared war on Germany on April 6, 1917. Immediately, armed forces were needed to accomplish the task. Congress knew that 1 million troops would be difficult to muster up on a volunteer basis, especially to fight an enemy on another continent. So about a month after the declaration of war, the Selective Draft Act of 1917 was passed by the House on May 16; by the Senate on May 17; and signed into law on May 18, 1917 by President Woodrow Wilson. It authorized the president to move the National Guard and Reserves into the regular army, and draft additional recruits as necessary to increase the number of ground troops to at least 1.2 million, and as high as 1.7 million. Included in the bill were provisions to prosecute any person who failed to register, failed to show up for induction, or deserted: 5 years prison plus up to $10,000 fine (a large sum at that time).

Along with the draft came protest. The American Union against Militarism was formed in November 1915 to counter Wilson's military preparedness campaign. The AUAM charged that conscription "ran counter to American values of individual initiative and freedom."

It is no surprise that about 15% of military-age Americans (3 million) failed to register; and almost 360,000 who received an induction notice either never showed up for induction, or else deserted after arriving at boot camp. War hysteria pervaded American society and such anti-war protesters and non-registrants were labeled German sympathizers or traitors. By mid-1918, about 10,000 non-registrants were arrested and prosecuted, and half of those who evaded induction or deserted were apprehended. The non-registrants claimed that conscription was not constitutional. They argued that congressional power to declare war and to raise armies did not include the authority to enact a conscription law and compel military service, and was also a violation of the 13th amendment (involuntary servitude). And they had a point, because the only one other occasion of conscription was during the Civil War (mentioned above) and which resolution by the Courts was vague and shallow.

The issue went to the Supreme Court under the heading of *Selective Service Draft cases*, and the pivotal case which set the precedent for all others was Arver et. al. versus United States, 245 US 366 (1918). Joseph F. Arver and others refused to register for the draft on June 5, 1917, and were subsequently tried and sentenced to 1 year in prison, and at the end of their term, they were to be conscripted into the armed forces.

By a unanimous vote the Supreme Court upheld the constitutionality of the Draft Act of 1917. Chief Justice Edward D. White wrote the court opinion (only the first paragraph is quoted).

> The grant to Congress of power to raise and support armies, considered in conjunction with the grants of the power to declare war, to make rules for the government and regulations of the land and naval forces, and to make laws necessary and proper for executing granted powers (Constitution, Art. 1, Sec. 8), includes the power to compel military service, exercised by the Selective Draft Law of May 18, 1917, c. 15, 40 Stat. 76. This conclusion, obvious upon the face of the Constitution, is confirmed by an historical examination of the subject.[234]

For the Supreme Court to rubber stamp the Draft Act was no surprise to anyone. Subsequent court cases of individuals who failed to register for the draft or who failed to be inducted, all of whom claimed that conscription was a power not permitted or delegated by the Constitution, were never heard by the Supreme Court. The courts have upheld the constitutionality of conscription during World War 2, Korea, and Vietnam, based on the decision of the above case.

---

[234] US Supreme Court, 245 US 366, affirmed January 7, 1918.

83 THE MILITARY CHAPLAINCY

Because the Constitution forbids legislation of laws prohibiting the establishment of religion or a resident's freedom to practice their religion, to resolve the conflict between conscience and the state regarding military service the state adopts the advice of Plato, the Greek philosopher, and implements an artificial religion for the residents of the state in the churches of its domain. The state in adopting this definition and use of God does not become Christian, but becomes the materialization of Plato's *Republic*. Religion implemented by the state surfaces in the form of the military chaplaincy and base chapels. "For God and Country," is the motto of Plato's secular religion. A person accepting this new religion now concludes that military service in obedience to the state has been approved by God the supreme authority, and is right and commendable. A soldier now proceeds in battle convinced that God is on his side, and that the enemy of the state as defined by the government is also the enemy of God to be vanquished.

The US government provides its artificial religion in the form of the US Chaplain Corps, whose duty is to attend to "the religious, spiritual, moral and ethical needs of the U.S. Army"[235] and all of the armed forces. The Army chaplaincy will be utilized in this section, although all branches of the US armed forces have their own chaplain corps. The status of the chaplains is defined as follows:

> 4–3. Professional status of chaplains
> *a.* Army chaplains have a dual role as religious leaders and staff officers. Their duties are prescribed by law, DOD policy, Army regulations, religious requirements, and Army mission. In performing their duties, chaplains do not exercise command, but exercise staff supervision

---

[235] Army Regulation AR 165-1, par. 4-1(b)

and functional direction of religious support personnel and activities (title 10, United States Code, section 3581).

b. The chaplain is a qualified and endorsed clergy person of a DOD recognized religious denomination or faith group.

c. Chaplains are noncombatants and will not bear arms.

d. The proper title for a chaplain is "chaplain" regardless of military rank or professional title. When addressed in writing, the chaplains rank will be indicated in parentheses (see AR 25–50 and AR 600–20).[236]

Their responsibilities are also clearly defined (selections only):

4–4. Religious responsibilities

a. Chaplains are required by law to hold religious services for members of the command to which they are assigned, when practicable (10 USC 3547). Chaplains provide for religious support, pastoral care, and the moral and ethical well-being of the command.

d. When conducting religious services, a chaplain will wear the military uniform, vestments, or other appropriate attire established by church law or denominational practice; (chaplains scarf, stole, or tallit may be worn with the uniform) (see AR 670–1).

e. Chaplains are authorized to conduct rites, sacraments, and services as required by their respective denomination.

f. Upon command orders, chaplains will conduct or assist in arranging for burial services at the interring of members of the military service, retired military personnel, and other personnel as authorized by Army regulations, DOD policy, and applicable law.

---

[236] Army Regulation AR 165-1. par. 4-3

g. Chaplains may perform marriage ceremonies for authorized DOD personnel upon request IAW the laws of the state or county where the marriage is to take place, and if the requirements of the officiating chaplain's denomination and local standing operating procedures (SOP) are met. Chaplains may perform marriage ceremonies for DOD military personnel overseas only if the persons desiring to marry have complied with all applicable civil law requirements of the host nation, with the requirements of Army regulations and with any military command directives.

h. Military and patriotic ceremonies may require a chaplain to provide an invocation, reading, prayer, or benediction. Such occasions are not considered to be religious services. Chaplains will not be required to offer a prayer, if doing so would be in variance with the tenets or practices of their faith group.

j. Chaplains will provide religious support for confined personnel and Army personnel in foreign or civilian confinement facilities (see AR 190–9 and AR 190–47).

k. The chaplain is a teacher of religion and provides religious instruction. The chaplain is responsible to the commander for the religious education program. The staff chaplain will integrate the religious education efforts of subordinate chaplains in the CMRP.[237]

Members of the US Chaplain Corp are also members of the US Armed Forces and considered officers of that branch of the US Military.

a. Chaplains normally enter the active duty Army as members of either the USAR (United States Army Reserve) or ARNG (Army National Guard). Chaplains appointed must meet the requirements of their

---

[237] Army Regulation AR 165-1. par. 4-4

ecclesiastical endorsing agent, DOD 1304.19, AR 135-100, and this regulation. Upon appointment, chaplains represent their distinctive faith group and serve as commissioned officers in the United States Army.[238]

Of course, when chaplains enlist into the military they take the same oath of allegiance to the Constitution and the President as any other recruit. This oath of allegiance places the US government as his supreme authority, and the god of the secular religion of the state is defined by the state in terms of what is in the best interests of the state. The creation of a chaplain corps is the materialization of Plato's advice of the state having a god that will align itself with the interests and intents of the state. The purpose of the chaplain on the battlefield is to provide moral support and comfort for the soldier while he kills the enemy, and especially provide encouragement if other soldiers have been killed in action.

In reviewing the responsibilities of the chaplain in the Army Regulations noted above, nowhere is it permitted him to question the morality of war or the death, wounding, crippling or suffering of any innocents, or the amount of devastation that he is causing. As active-duty officers in the US Armed Forces, chaplains are not free to criticize publicly the policies of the US government or the President, who is Commander-in-Chief of the US Armed Forces.

84   WAR AND THE MILITARY CHAPLAINCY

In the light of the Gospel of the NT, the religion provided by the Chaplain Corps is fraudulent, because its purpose is to provide divine approval for actions, conduct and regulations that are opposite to the purpose of the gospel of Jesus Christ. The rite of communion for dying soldiers, or requiem for those who have

---

[238] Army Regulation AR 165-1. par. 8-2(a)

died in battle, provides divine approval for the war the soldier is part of. In essence, the Chaplain Corps is the Department of Religion of the US government, it is created in order to provide artificial divine approval of all the legislature of the US government, its policy and its conduct, and to provide divine approval to a military vocation and all the military campaigns of the US armed forces. The military chaplain, supposedly representing Christianity – the religion of the Prince of Peace – is an officer of the military and must at all times wear a military uniform. Such an institution represents the pinnacle of the integration of religion and state, or the subjection of religion to the interests of the state, and primarily Christianity, which is the dominating religion in the US Chaplain Corp. But a military chaplaincy is antithetical to the NT concept of the ministry and life of Jesus, the Prince of Peace. American Christendom follows the same pattern as the subjection of the church to the state by Emperor Constantine I, to provide a religion for his subjects that is aligned with the interests of the state. One blatant example is the words of the chaplain under General George Patton during the WW2 invasion of Europe, who was requested by the general to pray for a victory. The chaplain offered his petition including the words, "Oh Lord, give us the wisdom to find the bastards and the strength to pile on."[239]

Under the pressure of combat and orders from superior military commanders, soldiers often disregarded acceptable rules of engagement and committed immoral acts such as the deliberate execution of prisoners. It was not unusual for chaplains to capitulate under the same pressure to justify such atrocities.

> War psychologists regarded the killing of prisoners as so commonplace that they devised formulae for assuaging soldiers' subsequent feelings of guilt. Roughly two-fifths

---

[239] Bergen, Doris, *The Sword of the Lord: Military Chaplains from the First to the Twenty-First Century.* pg. 236.

(40%) of American army chaplains surveyed after the war said that they had regarded orders to kill prisoners as legitimate.[240]

The counterfeit cause of the US Chaplaincy during the Vietnam War was also apparent to many soldiers stationed there and in combat. Many soldiers resented them, because they overwhelmingly supported the war, even to the point of endorsing it in the name of religion. Soldiers noticed how chaplains would regularly bless troops, their combat missions, their guns and their killing. The chaplaincy failed to curb the many atrocities, such as the massacre at My Lai, and critics indicted the chaplains for their silence in the matter. The Chaplaincy likewise failed to curb the widespread alcohol and drug abuse among combat soldiers in Vietnam.[241] Many American antiwar clergy and protesters were not shy to vent their opinions of the US Chaplaincy as a means for selling war as divinely approved and capitulating to the demands of the secular state, knowing well that the Vietnam war was a political venture. CALCAV,[242] for example, criticized the US Chaplaincy in Vietnam for failing to exercise their responsibility by protesting the war and for preaching a military religion that legitimized war and the military. The United Church of Christ task force indicted chaplains for their identification with military values and goals and, by implication, abandoning their commitment to their calling and church. The denominations that some of chaplains were members of had even condemned the war as immoral and unjust. It was only apparent that the US Chaplaincy failed to exercise a restraining role in Vietnam.[243]

But it is not only the US Chaplaincy that has such regulations, but the German armies of both WW1 and WW2 also had

---

[240] Ferguson, Niall, *The War of the World*, pg. 545
[241] Bergen, pg. 236
[242] Clergy And Laymen Concerned About Vietnam.
[243] Loveland, pg. 155.

chaplains in the field and in the combat areas. During WW1, the Kaiser Administration had over 1,000 chaplains, and the majority of them were Lutheran.[244] The Third Reich German Army also had regulations regarding their military chaplaincy. The following is a quote from the 1941 German Army High Command for spiritual care:

> As in earlier wars, in this war too, the military chaplaincy is an important handmaid of the troop leadership: education the men to enthusiastic willingness to give their utmost including their very lives; training warriors who are ready to sacrifice and by so doing, contributing to the spiritual strength of the German soldier at the front.[245]

During WW2, Germans chaplains were just as hard at work providing morale to their troops as American chaplains were providing to theirs. The work of German chaplains from their end likewise provided divine approval for their war effort against the Allies, and increased the amount of warfare, rather than curbing it. Doris Bergen in her study on the German Reich chaplaincy during WW2 notes the following:

> Approximately one thousand clergymen, Protestant and Catholic, served the German military as chaplains during the Second World War. Like their counterparts elsewhere, they preached, administered the sacraments, soothed the sick and wounded, and buried the dead... In order to protect themselves from their detractors (Reich officials), military chaplains in the Third Reich labored to prove and reprove that they met a real need of the troops and boosted morale. Yet the more successfully they did so – and especially on the Eastern Front, it

---

[244] Bergen, pg. 132.
[245] Bergen, pg. 178.

appears, they were successful – the more they helped legitimate a war of annihilation. Merely the presence of chaplains, at sites of mass killing in Poland, Yugoslavia, Greece, Byelorussia, and Ukraine, offered German warriors the comforting illusion that despite the blood on their hands, they remained decent people, linked to a venerable religious tradition.[246]

Just as with US military chaplains, the German chaplains were under similar regulations, as ordered by the officials of the German state. They were also to provide divine approval of their war effort, which only caused more death and devastation. The enigma in the situation is that denominational clergymen were providing religious comfort and support to both sides of the battlefield, and especially that both Lutheran and Catholic clergy were enlisted as chaplains in the military of both German and American armies.

85 THE CONSTITUTIONALITY OF THE CHAPLAIN CORPS

The one case that challenged the US Chaplain Corps to declare it unconstitutional was lost, but the plaintiff's argument was able to prove the validity of their claim, because the suit forced some changes in the administration of the US Chaplain Corp. As with the challenge regarding the constitutionality of conscription, this case was lost not because of their inadequate dispute or the illegality of their arguments, but because the military needed a chaplaincy for its success, and so the courts decided in their favor. The US Chaplaincy was also historically part of the US armed forces since the Continental Congress established it on July 29, 1775.

The plaintiffs were 2 law students, Joel Katcoff and Allen Wieder, whose suit was originally part of a research study or

---

[246] Bergen, pg.166

brief that they presented to the faculty of the Harvard Law School as part of their graduate dissertation. Then they proceeded to file a lawsuit using the results of their research against the Secretary of the Army. Katcoff and Wieder argued that the Chaplaincy program constituted an establishment of religion by the state in violation of the First Amendment, and that it was illegal for the state to utilize public funds – taxes – to support the chaplaincy, since it was directed only to specific religions that were approved by military officials.[247] The plaintiffs stated:

> "The United States government by design and appearance lends its prestige, influence and power to organized religion by granting commissions, rank and uniform to Army Chaplains."[248]

The other important argument of the plaintiffs was that the Military Commander had the ultimate responsibility for the Army's religious program, and not any of the chaplains or the Chief of Chaplains.[249] This was directly a violation of the First Amendment.

The defense of the military was that the chaplaincy program was a fulfillment of the clause in the First Amendment that stated "the free exercise thereof...," meaning that the chaplaincy program was a method of providing worship services to members of the armed forces. Their defense argued:

> "The Institution and Maintenance of the Chaplains Corps is Important to the National Defense, and is a Valid and Necessary Exercise of Congressional War Power."[250]

---

[247] United States District Court for the Eastern District Court of New York, Joel Katcoff and Allen M. Wieder, Plaintiffs, against Clifford L. Alexander, Jr., Secretary of the Army, and the Department of Defense, Defendants. Civil Action 79C-2986, November 23, 1979.
[248] ibid
[249] Army Regulation AR 165-1, par. 1-16(b)

The arguments of the military were only so obvious: unless the state had a means of providing divine approval to the military and its campaigns, it would have a difficult time obtaining recruits who would make good soldiers willing to kill and die on the battlefield. Of course, the courts could not rule in favor of the plaintiffs, the Chaplain Corps having been established in 1775 by the Continental Congress, and so it ruled in favor of the defense.

> In August 1980, Judge Mishler published his opinion. He supported the plaintiffs' standing as taxpayers, and stated that the court did have jurisdiction to review the case. He also noted that sometimes the Establishment Clause must accommodate the Free Exercise Clause, particularly in the unique military environment. It appeared from the Judge's comments that the constitutionality of the Chaplaincy extended only so far as it supported the soldier's free exercise of religion. Whatever went beyond meeting free exercise rights was subject to review and possible prohibition.[251]

Katcoff and Wieder appealed several times, but the verdict and conclusion of the matter never changed. In 1986, they decided to drop the case. The important item to note in this challenge is the validity of the plaintiff's suit, which was the illegal incorporation of religion into the military environment.

---

[250] quoted from Brinsfield, John W., *Encouraging Faith, Supporting Soldiers, the United States Army Chaplaincy, 1975-1996.*
[251] Brinsfield, ibid.

86 THE MINISTERIAL EXEMPTION

The exemption of the Christian clergy from secular responsibilities and a grant of special privileges that was not applied to the layperson or residents of the nation in general were first established by Constantine the Great.

> Constantine exalted the clergy. In A.D. 313, he gave the Christian clergy exemption from paying taxes—something that pagan priests had traditionally enjoyed. He also made them exempt from mandatory public office and other civic duties. They were freed from being tried by secular courts and from serving in the army.[252]

This exemption was not new, but Constantine was granting to them an immunity that had long been extended to pagan clergy.[253] The exemption was provided to the clergy because of the 2-tier attitude of the state toward clergy: the man of God must not stain his hands with blood, while the typical parishioner is not considered a man of God in the same manner as a clergyman, and due to the special superficial ordination that the man of God receives in order to be able to perform his rites and for his rites to be effective. The idea of having a man of God with blood on his hands would make the rites that he performs ineffective; it would no longer place him on a plateau above his parishioners closer to God, but equate him with the base individual who performs killing, just like an executioner. Who would want an executioner as the man of God to look up to in your congregation. The second aspect is the obligation of the clergyman to the state for the state allowing him this automatic exemption. The state impresses on the man of God the source of his religious freedom, and the state expects something in return. The clergyman's

---

[252] Viola, Frank, *Pagan Christianity;* Schaff, Philip, *History of the Christian Church,* vol. 3, chap. 1, section 1.
[253] Nicene and Post-Nicene Fathers, vol. 1, page 383, footnote 1.

support of state polity is expected, and especially the war that the clergyman is now exempt from participating in, from staining his hands in blood.

This enigma prevails in the exemption of religious ministers in the Selective Service System, which is IV-D, (defined in the Military Selective Service Act, 50 USC Appendix 456 g1),and also II-D (Appendix 456 g2), who are full-time students at a theological school or in preparation for the ministry. The logic is perplexing at best. If a person is a full-time minister of God, of in training, he is exempt from killing. The classification is not dependent on the tenets of the particular denomination that the priest, minister or rabbi is affiliated with or a member of. The tenets of the religion can be very militarists, such as the Mormon, Catholic, and most mainline and Evangelical Christian denominations. The parishioners of their respective congregations would not be exempt from military service, without proving themselves conscientious objectors, but their priest, minister or rabbi is automatically.

One psychologist, Willard Gaylin, MD, that studied the issue after interviewing several students at the Union Theological Seminary, New York, who were ministerial students to avoid the Vietnam draft, concluded the following:

> If it is said that a minister is a man of peace, so should it be said that he is a pastor, a leader. If it is against the teachings of God and church for man to kill, it is against the teaching for all men to kill. If a minister believers that his relationship with God will not permit him to bear arms, he should be required in the same manner that any man does to declare himself a conscientious objector and prove to a local draft board the sincerity of his this conviction. He cannot merely state that it is against his religious belief, for if it is against his religious belief it should be against the religious belief of every member of his flock. Historically, at any rate, the

churches have never found war the anathema that one theoretically would have assumed they would.[254]

During the Vietnam War, on April 17, 1967, 101,500 men were classified as IV-D. It was not unusual for many to register in theological schools in order to acquire a II-D exemption as a ministerial student.

87   THE BETRAYAL OF THE PRINCE OF PEACE BY MILITARIST CHRISTENDOM

This betrayal lies in the situation of churches of Christendom refusing to return to the original gospel message of Jesus Christ, generation after generation. Every generation betrays and crucifies the Prince of Peace when it continues to subject the gospel to the state and secular authority.

> Again the devil took him to a very high mountain and showed him all the kingdoms of the world and their glory of them, and he said to him, "All these I will give you, if you will fall down and worship me." Matt 4:8-9.

This is the temptation that confronts every child of God, and especially those in the circles of ecclesiastical influence: minister, pastor, priest, student and scholar. The betrayal occurs when the Christian gives divine support and approval to the work of the kingdoms of this world that contradict the law of God and gospel of the Prince of Peace, rather than resisting the temptation. To compromise the gospel and redefine it in terms of the kingdoms of this world is to capitulate to the devil, and the temporal rewards are many. These ministers are wardens over churches that are massive architectural monuments; they receive the respect of powerful secular rulers and military officials; they

---

[254] Gaylin, Willard, *In the Service of their Country: War Resisters in Prison*, pg. 268.

receive an income from the healthy donations of wealthy parishioners; they acquire the popularity of a large congregation; they accumulate considerable control over real estate and financial assets. This is Christendom, not Christianity. This new Christian church is redefined in terms of the needs of the state and society that the church is part of. Once the political policy is defined and established, the purpose of Christendom is the divine approval of its preservation, with each congregation becoming a national church in the country of its residency. As the state provides religious freedom, the congregation supports the dictates and needs of the state: this is Christendom, now itself a political force within the nation of its residency, ready to offer to it parishioners divine approval of the state polity and preservation of its civilization. But in exchange for freedom – saving their soul – they lose it due to their capitulation to the secular state.

Ecumenical Christendom is designed for a superficial adherence to the NT teachings, rather than a serious practice of the gospel. The practical issues of the NT, taught by Christendom, can be derived from most philosophers and humanists, and political leaders having a humanitarian nature, and the religion is supplemented with rites that are associated with the ministry of Jesus. But if theology and the shell of ecclesiastical sacerdotalism and sacraments were removed, the ethic and morality that would remain would essentially be no different than any that could not be derived from secular humanism, humanitarianism or philosophy. The idea of pacifism is not an issue to be seriously considered in the NT; it is fine and noteworthy during times of peace, for children's Sunday School lessons, and a precept to ponder, but not to be taken seriously, because it is only an ideal and impractical to actually implement. During wartime, Christendom as an institution becomes the state's department of religious services for the state, to echo and implement the requirements of the state. During war, so-called Christians do not conduct themselves any differently than people with no religious scruples or who are members of non-Christian religions. Essentially, there is nothing of substance or distinct about ecumenical Christendom once it is stripped of its superficial shell of ceremonialism, sacerdotalism and theology. The conclusion is that ecumenical Christendom denies the essence of the gospel that was preached by Jesus the Messiah, which was the deliverance of humanity from its perpetual self-destructive trend of warfare. The elimination of preparation and training for war, and its replacement by reconciliation, is the salvation that Jesus the Messiah came to provide his Jewish countrymen, and that toleration of abuse suffered in the process would be less devastating than aggression or reprisal suffered in war. Eventually this gospel was to extend to all nations, for them to convert their weapons into implements of agriculture and not to learn war anymore.

During war, industries produce employment and profits, and during war, many residents are employed in industries that are related to the war effort. Since ministers are supported by the charitable contributions of parishioners, they are not about to bite the hand that feeds them by dictating form their pulpit that such employment is antithesis to the gospel of the Prince of Peace, and that employment should be sought elsewhere for the Christian, in some vocation that is directly a benefit to society. It is almost treason and disloyalty for a minister to tell his parishioners not to be employed by a company designing, manufacturing, or selling weapons or military-related equipment and accessories. In no manner will ministers of mainline denominations be critical of war, if they expect to keep their pulpit and the respect of their parishioners.

Although the First Amendment states that the government will not respect any one religion over another, this is applicable only during peacetime. During wartime, the unwritten rule is the respect of those religions that defend the war from the pulpit and support the war effort by providing recruits for the armed forces from among the military-age parishioners of their congregations. Religions whose pulpits do not echo the voice of the state are deprived of freedom of speech and freedom of the press, and are suspected of treason and even collaboration with the enemy. The state requires approval of its dictates from national religious organizations and denominations to provide a united and formidable front without dissension against the enemy. In exchange for this, the state provides such groups religious freedoms – speech and the press – during wartime.

88   LEGITIMATE DISOBEDIENCE OF THE STATE

There are two examples in the OT of state officials refusal to obey commands issued by their head of state, even with the balance of officials of the state supporting the edict. These two examples serve as evidence that the Biblical injunction to obey state officials of Rom 13 is only valid as long as the edict does not violate or contradict the law of God. The state is comprised of individuals whose responsibility is the welfare of the population of the nation, but when these same officials legislate law that conflicts with the law of God, then they have exceeded the authority delegated to them, because, "there is no authority except from God." Rom 13:1. Any civil law that contradicts the law of God is not to the benefit of the population, because the law of God is to be the basis of all law that is legislated for the benefit of the nation.

In Dan 3 an event is described where King Nebuchadnezzar erects a gold statue of immense proportion: 90 feet high and 9 feet wide, and expects all his subjects to prostrate themselves before it. All comply with his request, until some of his officials inform him that 3 Jewish men who are also officials in his government refuse to do so. They tell the king, "These men, O king, pay no heed to you; they do not serve your gods or worship the golden image that you set up." Dan 3:12. Shadrach, Meshach, and Abednego are called to the presence of the king and reply to him, saying, "O Nebuchadnezzar, we have no need to answer you in this matter. If it be so, our God whom we serve is able to deliver us from the burning fiery furnace; and he will deliver us out of your hand, O king. But if not, be it known to you, O king, that we will not serve your gods or worship the golden image which you have set up." Dan 3:16-18.

These 3 men, even though they were officials of the government of Nebuchadnezzar, nonetheless refused to follow a law that they considered to be unjust, because it was in conflict with the law of God, not to venerate any images, the Second Commandment. The 3 were likewise willing to go to their death.

The second event is recorded in Dan 6, where Daniel refuses to obey the edict to only petition King Nebuchanezzar on any matter. Government officials manipulated the king to issue this edict, in order to find reason to discredit Daniel or perhaps have him terminated from his government post. But the authority of the state – the king and his officials who legislated this law – is not above the authority of the living God, and so Daniel proceeded to ignore the edict and continued to pray to the God of heaven in his customary manner. After his arrest for violating this edict, Daniel was willing to go to his death, rather than capitulate to the officials and the edict of the state.

The contemporary Christian pacifist may have to proceed in the same manner, if he is placed in that position where the state requires him to violate the command of Jesus Christ the Prince of Peace by conscripting him into the armed forces. Just as Daniel, Shadrach, Meshach, and Abednego refused to comply with an unjust edict, because it was in conflict with the law of God, the contemporary Christian will have to do the same, and likewise be willing to refuse even if it means his own death. The example provided for us is Jesus Christ himself, who went to his death without defending himself before the Sanhedrin.

PART NINE

THE CONTEMPORARY CHRISTIAN PACIFIST

The Church could turn the world toward peace if every congregation lived and taught as Jesus lived and taught.
John Stoner

89 THE CHRISTIAN PACIFIST OF TODAY

The Christian pacifist is a conscientious objector to war in any form, and to military service and training, because he is a disciple of Jesus Christ the Son of God and Prince of Peace and conducts himself based on the precepts he taught.

The disciple of Jesus Christ considers war organized and premeditated murder on an international scale. It is controlled criminal insanity resulting in violence and devastation, and without justification. They recognize that the purpose of military training is to make men killing machines. There is only one manner for the disciple of Jesus Christ to conduct himself in regard to the question of military service and that is to refuse. The conscience of the true Christian will prohibit them from such participation, and which includes employment manufacturing military equipment and weapons.

A person who claims to be Christian and is faced with the dilemma of whether to enlist in the military should contemplate in the following terms, "Will my service in the military institute peace, or will it promote more war and aggression? Is the military a service unto the living God, or is it service unto the secular god of war? If I die in combat, do I die for a purpose that is worth the value of my life, or do I die as a pawn of the state? Do I acknowledge as supreme the dictates of the secular state, or those of the spiritual kingdom? Should I suffer on the battlefield as a sacrifice to the state, or should I suffer for my faith as a Christian?"

A Christian is a pacifist in these terms. "My convictions will not allow me to participate in military service, armed combat, or any aggression. Jesus of Nazareth, the son of God, taught pacifism as part of his gospel of the Kingdom. He exemplified in his personal life and ministry that I am not to retaliate or take vengeance for any injury committed against me or against another person or society. even if it means my own injury or death. The gospels teach that further aggression does not resolve conflict. I cannot face the judgment seat of Christ knowing that I have taken the life of a soldier or an innocent person, or destroyed property in war, or caused people to suffer. I will not have a clean conscience if I am employed manufacturing military equipment or weapons. Although I am in the world, I am not of the world."

The Christian pacifist is an enigma in society. He is an enigma as well in the ecclesiastical world. The most popular cliché, "Anything worth having is worth fighting for," does not apply to the Christian pacifist, because the entirety of the material world is temporal as a result of the short life span of the individual. There is nothing so valuable or indispensable that it is necessary for the Christian pacifist to use violence or weapons to defend it or retain it. The philosophy of the Christian pacifist makes him distinct from the balance of other individuals: he refuses to utilize force or violence or weapons under any circumstances to prove his convictions, defend himself or his Christian faith or congregation, or to compel any person to do his will, even if it means the loss of his property, mortal or physical harm, deprivation of freedom, or even the loss of his own life.

The Christian pacifist is an enigma in the realm of ecumenical Christendom because his interpretation of the message of the New Testament is diametrically opposite to the popular and historical one. The Christian pacifist is smaller than a miniscule minority, yet his presence unleashes considerable upheaval in military recruitment and conscription. The true believer embarrasses the recruits of Christian denominations because he forces them to reevaluate their decision to join the military and subject themselves to military training in the light of the gospel of the person they claim to accept and believe as Prince of Peace. The true believer forces the "Christian" soldier to realize that perhaps the salvation of Jesus is salvation from war, that by taking the same course of non-violence as did Jesus, no more suffering and dearth and devastation will occur. The true believer forces the "Christian" recruit to consider that the oath of allegiance to the secular state he took when he joined the armed forces was a capitulation to the kingdoms of this world, and a denial of the denial of the divine kingdom; that he was affirming the authority of the state over the authority of the Gospel; that he replaced his loyalty to Jesus King of kings with loyalty to the supreme head of the secular state.

Viewing the matter from another aspect, how can a person be converted, led to accept Jesus as their savior, be reborn, if that person is burned at the stake as a heretic or executed in the name of God, or killed on the battlefield, or destroyed or maimed by a bomb dropped on them from a jet bomber flown by a Christian? It is impossible to be both patriotic and nationalistic and spiritual at the same time. A person can only have one supreme master on any matter, or legislator that he will subject himself to as the final authority.

90 CHRISTIAN RESPONSIBILITY TO THE STATE

There are 2 passages in the New Testament that deal with the obedience of the Christian to the state and the role of the security force or police. The era that these passages were written was that of Nero Caesar, Emperor 54-68 AD. He was the most inhumane and ruthless of any emperor during the 1st century AD. The apostles in their inspired letters to believers disregard the evil of the person himself and focus rather on the intent of government, which is to provide a civil framework for the success of the society and for the security and safety of the residents.

> Let every person be subject to the governing authorities. For there is no authority except from God, and those that exist have been instituted by God. Therefore he who resists the authorities resists what God has appointed, and those who resist will incur judgment. For rulers are not a terror to good conduct, but to bad. Would you have no fear of him who is in authority? Then do what is good and you will receive his approval, for he is a servant of God for your good. But if you do wrong, be afraid for he does not bear the sword in vain; he is the servant of God to execute his wrath on the criminal. Therefore one must be subject, not only to avoid God's wrath but also for the sake of conscience. For the same reason you also pay taxes, for the authorities are ministers of God, attending to this very thing. Pay all of them their dues, taxes to whom taxes are due, revenue to whom revenue is due, respect to whom respect is due, honor to whom honor is due. Rom 13:1-7.

> Be subject for the sake of the Lord to every human institution, whether it be to the emperor as supreme, or to governors as sent by him to punish those who do wrong and to praise those who do right. 1 Pet 2:13-14.

Apostle Paul prefaces his passage by stating that the concept of government is divine, meaning that the motivation to establish a ruling body over the population for civil purposes is based on a correct understanding of the intention of God for humanity. But also notice in verse 4, the statement that the state was made for people, and not the opposite. The state exists to serve its subjects, not vice versa, meaning that the state's purpose is to protect its residents. The laws and legislation of the state are the dictates of a corporate body of individuals such as ourselves to whom we have allocated authority. Unconditional obedience to the state cannot be reconciled with the doctrine of the absolute sovereignty of God. The priority must be given to God, as Peter and the apostles stated, "We must obey God rather than men." Acts 5:29.

The political task of the state has 2 aspects: the negative, which is to preserve society from anarchy and social disruption by restraining crime, and usually through a police force. The state limits the damage caused by the sin of criminals, having the authority granted to it by God to impose a penalty on individuals who commit a crime. Although morals cannot be legislated, nonetheless, laws restrain people from injuring themselves and others. By instituting a penal system, the state permits society to prosper with the least amount of disruption and crime. The statement by Apostle Paul that the civil servant carries a sword to be utilized is to be understood as the responsibility of the state to provide safety and security for the population.

The second task of the state is positive: to provide an environment that will allow the economy and infrastructure to develop.

There is no justification for a Christian to violate the laws of the state that are designed for the security and prosperity of the population. There is nothing to be gained in protests, demonstrations or violent civil disobedience. Any violation of just laws discredits the Christian religion. Christians must be especially good examples of moral conduct so others may recognize the value and blessing of being a disciple of Jesus Christ. Both apostles Peter and Paul impress upon the Christian the necessity for respect of civil authority. The Christian is to be complemented as a law abiding citizen and benefit to the society.

91   CHRISTIAN PACIFISM AND THE STATE

Pacifism does not weaken the defense of a country. The tendency to be attacked is reduced if a country is non-pretentious in the worldview. Countries will be more conducive to peaceful relations if neither has an army. By joining the armed forces of your particular country, the military strength necessarily increases and such an increase contributes to an arms race in neighboring and distant countries. A country noticing arms and military development in its neighbor will sense the necessity of increasing its own military strength suspicious of his neighbor's intents. Increase of armaments increases the suspicions of neighboring countries that would not otherwise come to such conclusions, thereby increasing arms themselves, and perhaps even attacking their neighbor, thinking that their neighbor is preparing to do the same – a pre-emptive attack. A powder-keg is created once both neighbors are saturated with weapons, and only a spark is required to ignite the powder and initiate war. Any preparation for war creates an environment conducive to war, whether this is intended or not, and this will easily precipitate war. Such occurred in Europe in the years prior to World War 1.

In the process, peace movements are stifled and discredited, politicians and patriotic citizens accuse anti-war protestors of being traitors and clandestine supporters of the enemy. Patriots claim that such peace efforts bolster the enemy's strength by psychologically reducing the vigilance of their own national military. In reality, such extreme patriotism creates a windfall of arms supply and interferes with any possible reconciliation efforts to curb or preclude combat, now the inevitable. The best way of avoiding war is not to prepare for it, because preparations for war hasten war.

Even if a nation develops an attitude of militant imperialism and attacks another country, the least amount of defense, reprisal or vengeance will reduce the number of casualties. True that many will suffer and die in the process of the invasion, but the overall amount will be reduced if the residents of the invaded country conduct themselves non-pretentiously; turning the cheek, loving their enemy, putting down their weapon, not living by the sword. The difficulty in taking this approach is the prevailing attitude of nationalism, it is the patriotic rhetoric of "Give me liberty or give me death." The NT teaches of harmony and submission, not an attitude of vendetta toward oppressors. If a person's attitude is peaceful coexistence between the occupation army and subjected residents, then their existence will be tolerable, and at least no revolt or revolutionary war will cause additional loss of lives or destruction of property. Robert Holmes, a professor of philosophy, describes this in the words:

> A people committed to non-violence may be deprived of their government, their liberties, their material wealth, even their lives. But they cannot be conquered. True, non-violence could be effective on such a scale, only with the concerted effort of tens of thousands of well-trained persons willing to sacrifice and perhaps die for what they believe in.[255]

People who seek security by relying on military force are emasculated of their defense once their military is defeated. This utilization of myriads of soldiers in warfare has been tested for successive generations over the millennia and has only created a self-perpetuating trend of destruction, while at least with the approach of non-violence and self-sacrifice, the amount of death and devastation will be substantially reduced, and with the possibility of the conversion of the occupying nation to peace.

The extent of civil obedience is defined by Jesus in a conversation with Herodians, residents of Judea who had political affiliation with the family of Herod the Great.

---

[255] Holmes, Robert, *On War and Morality*, pg. 273-274.

"Tell us what you think. It is lawful to pay taxes to Caesar or not?" But Jesus, aware of their malice, said, "Why put me to the test, you hypocrites? Show me the money for the tax." And they brought him a coin. Jesus said to them, "Whose likeness and inscription is this?" They said, "Caesar's." Then he said to them, "Render therefore to Caesar what is Caesar's, and to God what is God's." Matt 21:17-21.

This passage can be interpreted in the following manner in the light of the earlier passages by the apostle regarding civil obedience. The reimbursement to the state for the privilege of living in this country is payment of taxes and obedience of civil law. The line of obedience is drawn when the state requires a person to sacrifice their life for the country they reside in. At this point the state is usurping authority over life which only belongs to God the author of life. The state in demanding the life of a person installs itself as deity, and which is a capacity beyond that which the Bible rightfully attributes to and allows the state. This is the right of the Christian, to refuse to yield to the state what belongs to God, their allegiance and life.

The Christian is only a pilgrim and spiritual migrant in this world, a temporal resident, a person traveling through the valley of earthly experience on their journey to the eternal kingdom. The apostles wrote regarding this in the following:

These all died in faith, not having received what was promised, but having seen it and greeted if from afar, and having acknowledged that they were strangers and exiles on the earth. Heb 11:13.

Beloved, I beseech you as aliens and exiles to abstain from the passions of the flesh that wage war against you soul. I Pet 2:11.

Because of this the Christian does not become involved in the politics of secular government. These are matters that envelop the personality of a political figure and more than often do not pertain to issues. Christian involvement in government should always pertain to issues of a moral and ethical nature. What is important an individual should accomplish with their own family and associates and their religious community. Involvement in politics tends to direct the sight of the spiritual migrant away from the eternal kingdom and to the temporal issues of the state.

The one unanswerable question proposed often to the conscientious objector by advocates of defense and retaliation is the following, "What would you do if somebody attacked your wife or mother or child in your presence?" A concrete answer cannot be offered because nobody actual knows what they will do in such a situation. The sincere Christian will only state that they hope they will react in such a manner to curb the attack, or not cause any more injury, or perhaps sacrifice their own safety to protect the other person.

91   WHAT NEEDS TO BE DONE

True and genuine Christians, disciples of Jesus of Nazareth, must refuse participation in war in any form. Priests and ministers must corporately voice to their congregations for their members to not enlist in the military, to refuse conscription and participation in war, and to not have a vocation in the manufacture of weapons and munitions. Only the Christian Church can stop the tide of the devastating results of war and military aggression by taking this stand. Only by returning to its Apostolic roots can the Christian Church fulfill its responsibility to its founder Jesus of Nazareth, who said, "Put down that sword Peter, for whoever takes the sword will perish by the sword." First and foremost priests and ministers must be willing to lay down their life in imitation of Jesus Christ as an example to others, instead of condoning, advocating or further contributing to war and devastation. Peace is the way to terminating the existence of war, even if it entails suffering or martyrdom, as with the example provided by Jesus the Son of God in his earthly career.

Go to your minister and priest and elder and tell them, "It's time for our congregation to return to our Apostolic roots and adhere to the gospel as taught by our founder Jesus of Nazareth, Messiah of Israel, and to withdraw that weapon from use. It's time to become a peace church, to teach religious objection to the military in our congregation and for all the members to refuse to have a vocation in a military-related industry."

It is difficult to be a conscientious objector because you are in the minority and are liable to be labeled a traitor, a coward, unpatriotic, and not willing to serve your country as others have done in the wars of previous generations. The choice is a difficult one and Jesus knew that it would not be easy, just as he said, "If any person will follow me, let him deny himself and take up his cross and follow me." Matt 16:24. Others have suffered and the contemporary true Christian must realize that he may have to also. The true Christian must have the attitude that he or she would rather die and lose his life rather than contribute to war and military aggression. This can be accomplished due to their belief in their resurrection from death: that if they die for the principles of the Gospel of Christ, they will resurrect at His second advent. True Christians do not fear death, because it is the transition to eternal life. Others have suffered and the contemporary true Christian must realize that he may have to also. It is this faith that will lead to the termination of war, and likewise enlighten the population, cease aggression, and serve as an example to others, and especially those of future generations to curb war entirely and eventually.

BIBLIOGRAPHY:

Abrams, Ray H., *Preachers Present Arms*, Herald Press, Scottdale, PA, 1969

Anderson, Richard C. *Peace was in their Hearts: Conscientious Objectors in World War 2*, Correlan Publications, 1994

Augustine of Hippo, *The City of God*, translated by Marcus Dods, The Modern Library, New York, 2000.

Bacevich, Andrew J, *The New American Militarism: How Americans are Seduced by War*, Oxford University Press, 2005

Bainton, Roland H. *Christian Attitudes toward War and Peace*, Abingdon Press, Nashville, TN, 1960

Ballou, Adin, *Christian Non-Resistance*, Blackstone Editions, 203

Ballou, Adin, *Practical Christianity*, Blackstone Editions, 203

Bergen, Doris, L., Ed. *The Sword of the Lord: Military Chaplains from the First to the Twenty-First Centuries*, University of Notre Dame Press, Notre Dame, IN. 2004

Boettner, Loraine, *The Christian Attitude Toward War*, Presbyterian and Reformed Publishing Conpany, Phillipsburg, NJ, 1985

Bourke, Joanna, *An Intimate History of Killing*, Basic Books, 1999.

Brock, Peter, *A Brief History of Pacifism from Jesus to Tolstoy*, Syracuse University Press, 1992

Brock, Peter, *Freedom from Violence: Sectarian Nonresistance from the Middle Ages to the Great War*, University of Toronto Press, 1991.

Brock, Peter, *Pacifism in the United States from the Colonial Era to the First World War*, Princeton University Press, Princeton, NJ, 1968.

Brown, Peter, *Augustine of Hippo*, University of California Press, 1967.

Cadoux, John C., *The Early Christian Attitude to War*, Seabury Press, New York, 1982

Cantine, Holly, and Rainer, Dachine, *Prison Etiquette*, Southern Illinois University Press, 1950
Carpinter, Alvin L. *From Missionary to Mercenary*, iUniverse, New York. 2005
Catechism of the Catholic Church, Liguori Publications, 1994.
Chambers, John Whiteclay II, *To Raise an Army: The Draft comes to Modern America*, The Free Press, 1987.
Christie-Murray, David, *A History of Heresy*, Oxford University Press, 1976.
Clausewitz, Carl von, *On War*, Penguin Books, 1968
Codevilla, Angelo and Seabury, Paul, *War: Ends and Means*, Potomac Books, Washington, DC, 2006.
Cole, Darrell, *When God says War is Right*, Waterbrook Press, 2002.
Cornwell, John, *Hitler's Pope: The Secret History of Pius XII*, Viking Books, 1999.
Cowley, Robert, Ed. *Experience of War*, Laurel Books, 1992
Drescher, John M. *Why I am a Conscientious Objector*, Masthof Press, 2001.
Duffy, Michael K. *Peacemaking Christians*, Sheed and Ward, Kansas City, KS,1995
Duggan, Joseph C. *The Legislative and Statutory Development of the Federal Concept of Conscription for Military Service*, The Catholic University of America Press, Washington DC, 1946
Dyer, Gwynne, *War: The Lethal Custom*, Carroll and Graf, New York, 2004.
Dymond, Johnathan, *An Inquiry into the Accordancy of War with the Principles of Christianity*, William Wood and Co. 1870.
Ferguson, John, *The Politics of Love: The New Testament and Nonviolent Revolution*, Fellowship Publications, Nyack, New York 1979.
Ferguson, John, *War and Peace in the World's Religions*, Sheldon Press, London, 1977.
Ferguson, Niall, *The War of the World*, Penguin Books, 2006

Fitzpatrick, Edward, A. *Conscription and America*, Richard Publishing Company, Milwaukee, WI, 1940

Frazer, Heather T. and O'Sullivan, John, *We have just began to not Fight: An Oral History of Conscientious Objectors in Civilian Public Service during World War II*, Twayne Publishers, 1996

Freeman, Charles, *The Closing of the Western Mind*, Vintage Books, 2002.

Gaylin, Dr. Willard, *In the Service of their Country: War Resisters in Prison*, The Viking Press, 1970

Glover, Jonathan, *Humanity: A Moral History of the Twentieth Century*, Yale University Press, 2000.

Grossman, Dave, *On Killing*, Little, Brown and Company, 1995

Hallock, Daniel, *Hell, Healing and Resistance: Veterans Speak*, Plough Publishing House, 1998.

Harnack, Adolf, *Militia Christi, The Christian Religion and the Military in the First Three Centuries*, Fortress Press, Philadelphia, PA, 1963

Hedges, Chris, *War is a Force that Gives us Meaning*, Anchor Books, 2003.

Heering, Gerrit Jan, *The Fall of Christianity: A Study of Christianity, the State and War*, translated by J.W. Thompson, Fellowship Publications, 1943

Helgeland, John, Ed. *Christians and the Military, The Early Experience*, Fortress Press, Philadelphia, PA, 1985

Hershberger, Guy Franklin, *War, Peace and Nonresistance*, Herald Press, Scottdale, PA, 1981

Holmes, Robert L, *On War and Morality*, Princeton University Press, 1989.

Holy Bible, various translations.

Horsh, John, *The Principle of Nonresistance as held by the Mennonite Church*, Eastern Mennonite Publications, 1985.

Jones, Rufus, M. Ed, *The Church, the Gospel and War*, Harper and Brothers, 1948.

Kaplan, Esther, *With God on their Side, George W. Bush and the Christian Right*, The New Press, 2005.

Keegan, John, *A History of Warfare*, Vintage Books, 1994

Keim, Albert N., *The CPS Story, An Illustrated History of Civilian Public Service,* Good Books, 190

Kellogg, Walter Guest, *The Conscientious Objector*, Boni and Liveright, 1919.

Kohn, Stephen M. *Jailed for Peace: The History of American Draft Law Violators, 1658-1985*, Greenwood Press, Westport, CT, 1986

Lassere, Jean, *War and the Gospel,* translated by Oliver Coburn, Herald Press, Scottdale, PA. 1998

Latourette, Kenneth Scott, *A History of Christianity, Volume 1.* Harper and Row, San Francisco, CA.1975.

Lewis, Clive Staples, *The Weight of Glory*, Harper San Francisco, 2001.

Loveland, Anne, C. *American Evangelicals and the U.S. Military 1942-1993*, Louisiana State University Press, Baton Rouge, LA. 1996

Lynd, Alice, *We Won't Go: Personal Accounts of War Objectors*, Beacon Press, Boston, 1968

Martin, William, *A Prophet with Honor: The Billy Graham Story*, William Morrow and Co. New York, 1991.

McCarthy, Emmanuel Charles, *Christian Just War Theory: The Logic of Deceit*, Center for Christian Nonviolence

McNeill, William H. *The Pursuit of Power*, The University of Chicago Press, 1982

McSorley, Richard, *New Testament Basis of Peacemaking*, Herald Press, Scottdale, PA, 1985

Merton, Thomas, *The Seven Story Mountain*, 1976, Harcourt, Brace and Company, New York.

Miller, Melissa and Shenk, Phil M., *Path of Most Resistance: Mennonite Conscientious Objectors who did not Co-Operate with the Vietnam War Draft*, Herald Press, 1982.

Murry, J. Middleton, *The Betrayal of Christ by the Churches*, Andrew Dakers Ltd. London, 1940

Musurillo, Herbert Anthony, *The Acts of Christian Martyrs*, Oxford University Press, 1972

Neibuhr, Reinhold, *Moral Man and Immoral Society*, Charles Scribner's Sons, New York, 1932

Nelson, Karl D. *By Reason of Religious Training and Belief: A History of Conscientious Objection and Religion during the Vietnam War*, dissertation presented to the Western Washington University.

Peachey, Paul, Ed. *Peace, Politics and the People of God*, Fortress Press, Philadelphia, PA, 1986

Peters, Shawn Francis, *Judging Jehovah's Witnesses: Religious Persecution and the Dawn of the Rights Revolution*, University Press of Kansas, 2000

Philo, *The Works of Philo*, translated by C.D. Yonge, Hendrickson Publishers, 1993.

Plato, *Republic*, translated by Benjamin Jowett, Barnes and Noble, 2004.

Rand, Ayn, *Capitalism, The Unknown Ideal*, Signet Books, 1967

Rehnquist, William H. *All the Laws but One: Civil Liberties in Wartime*, Vintage Books, 2000

Ropp, Theodore, *War in the Modern World*, The John Hopkins University Press, 2000

Runciman, Steven, *The Medieval Manichee*, Cambridge University Press, 1960.

Russell, Bertrand, *Why I am not a Christian and other essays*, Simon and Schuster, New York, 1957

Schaff, Philip, Ed. *Ante-Nicene Fathers*, Christian Literature Publishing Company, 1896

Schaff, Philip, Ed. *Nicene and Post-Nicene Fathers*, Second Series, Christian Literature Publishing Company, 1896.

Schaff, Philip, *History of the Christian Church*

Schlissel, Lilian, Ed. *Conscience in America, A Documentary History of Conscientious Objection in America 1757-1967*, E.P. Dutton and Company, 1968

Schurer, Emil, *A History of the Jewish People at the Time of Christ*, 5 volumes, Hendrickson Publishers, 1998.

Seeley, Robert, *Choosing Peace*, Central Committee for Conscientious Objectors, 1994.

Shubin, Daniel H., *Leo Tolstoy and the Kingdom of God within You*, 2009.
Shubin, Daniel H., *The Synodal Era and the Sectarians, History of Russian Christianity,* volume 3, Algora Publishing.
Sigmund, Paul E. Ed. *St. Thomas Aquinas on Politics and Ethics,* W.W. Norton and Company, 1988
Sittser, Gerald L. *A Cautious Patriotism: The American Churches and the Second World War,* University of North Carolina Press, 1997.
Snow, Michael, *Christian Pacifism, Fruit of the Narrow Way,* Friends United Press, Richmond, IN 1981
Sun-Tzu, *The Art of War*
Sweet, Leonard I., *The Lion's Pride: American and the Peaceable Community,* Abington Press, Nashville, TN, 1987.
Tollefson, James W. *The Strength not to Fight: An Oral History of Conscientious Objectors of the Vietnam War.* Little, Brown and Company, 1993.
Tolstoy, Leo, *The Kingdom of God is within You*, Noonday Press, 1975.
Tolstoy, Leo, *Writings on Civil Disobedience and Nonviolence*, New Society Publishers, 1987.
Trocme, Andre, *Jesus and the Nonviolent Revolution*, translated by Michael Shank and Marlin E. Miller, Herald Press, Scottdale, PA, 1998.
Vance, Laurence, *Christianity and War,* Vance Publications, Pensacola, FL, 2005.
Wittner, Lawrence S., *Rebels against War: The American Peace Movement* 1941-1960, Columbia University Press, 1969.
Yoder, John Howard, *The Politics of Jesus,* William B. Eerdman's Publishing Company, 2002.
Zaroulis, Nancy and Sullivan, Gerald, *Who Spoke Up? American Protest against the War in Vietnam, 1963-1975,* Holt, Rinehart and Winston, New York, 1984.
Zinn, Howard, *A People's History of the United States,* Harper Classics.

www.ingramcontent.com/pod-product-compliance
Lightning Source LLC
Chambersburg PA
CBHW032039150426
43194CB00006B/351